Symposia

BibleWorld
Series Editor: Philip R. Davies, University of Sheffield

BibleWorld shares the fruits of modern (and postmodern) biblical scholarship not only among practitioners and students, but also with anyone interested in what academic study of the Bible means in the twenty-first century. It explores our ever-increasing knowledge and understanding of the social world that produced the biblical texts, but also analyses aspects of the bible's role in the history of our civilization and the many perspectives – not just religious and theological, but also cultural, political and aesthetic – which drive modern biblical scholarship.

Published:

Forthcoming:

SYMPOSIA

Dialogues Concerning the History of Biblical Interpretation

Roland Boer

LONDON   OAKVILLE

Published by

UK: Equinox Publishing Ltd., Unit 6, The Village, 101 Amies St.,
London SW11 2JW
USA: DBBC, 28 Main Street, Oakville, CT 06779

www.equinoxpub.com

First published 2007

British Library Cataloguing-in-Publication Data

A catalogue record for this book is available from the British Library.

ISBN-10   1 84553 101 9 (hardback)
           1 84553 102 7 (paperback)

ISBN-13   978 1 84553 101 0 (hardback)
           978 1 84553 102 7 (paperback)

Library of Congress Cataloging-in-Publication Data

Boer, Roland, 1961-
  Symposia : dialogues concerning the history of biblical interpretation
Roland Boer.
    p. cm. — (Bibleworld)
  Includes bibliographical references and index.
  ISBN 1-84553-101-9 (hb) — ISBN 1-84553-102-7 (pb) 1.
Bible—Criticism, interpretation, etc.—History. I. Title. II. Series:
Bible world (London, England)
  BS500.B59 2006
  220.609—dc22

                                                        2006015883

Typeset by S.J.I. Services, New Delhi
Printed and bound in Great Britain by Lightning Source UK Ltd., Milton Keynes and in the
United States of America by Lightning Source Inc., La Vergne, TN

For George Aichele

CONTENTS

PREFACE

I must confess to having read Plato's *Symposium* only recently. Since I was writing a similarly titled book, indeed a book with a similar structure, I thought I had better read the original, even if it was some 2,400 years after it was written. Reading Plato is a bit like reading the Bible or indeed Marx: some bits we know very well, having absorbed them in ways in which we are barely conscious, and other bits we are surprised to find there at all. Many of the readers of this book might be able to tick some of the following: the myth of the cave; the theory of forms or ideas; the banishment of playwrights from his ideal republic; the philosopher king; Platonic relationships, to name but a few.

But then I may be assuming too much, since reading the *Symposium* took me back to my first degree in Classics: small classes, often just a couple of us, at the University of Newcastle (the Australian version) set in the delta of the coal-bound Hunter Valley. With all my teenage friends heading off to take up apprenticeships in the mines, or, if they finished high school, foreman's positions at the same mines where they still earn way more than I ever will, no one could make sense of Classics. I was doing it, I would say over a drink, to prepare myself for the day when time machines were invented and the immigration department desperately suddenly needs interpreters for travellers and migrants from ancient Greece, Rome and India.

Greek and Latin were piles of fun: eccentric professors who were correspondents with J.R.R. Tolkien, who smoked pipes and held their large stomachs when they tried to explain the meaning of *gravitas* in Roman politics, who never ironed their clothes (and I mean the women), who turned up drunk at 11 am on *Friday morning* to parties that went over the whole weekend (again, I mean the women), who set us exam texts we had never seen before by mistake, apart from the actual 'unseen' translation, who expected us to be able to compose not merely Latin and Greek prose but Latin and Greek *verse*, in metre.

Somewhat paradoxically, however, Sanskrit was my favourite. We met from eight until ten pm on Tuesdays and Thursdays with a worker from the steel mill, a single mother and a large gay mathematics teacher. The room would fill with cigarette smoke, we would drink endless small glasses of cheap sherry, courtesy of our professor, he would disappear to his room every now and then, still lecturing as he walked up and down the hallway, and we (amazingly) learnt some Sanskrit.

Godfrey Tanner was the professor of Classics. I tend to see him as Socrates even now and those classes in Sanskrit were the closest we ever came to Plato's *Symposium*, or as it should be, *Symposion*. In a steel and coal town, proud of its university, Godfrey made quite a splash. Questioning, putting forth new theories to test the waters, riding his bicycle between home and university while wearing his academic robes, thoroughly engrossed in the life of the university (they named a bar after him, a section of the library, a lecture series and a student fellowship), an avid member of the Anglican Cathedral for all the *wrong* reasons. The town joked about Godfrey, told stories of his antics, feared and revered him – Socrates indeed.

Quite some triggers for my memory tracks, then, in that reading of the *Symposium* as the wind freshened and whipped up the waters of Port Stephens. But what is the *Symposium* after all? A dinner-party – except that the English term conveys all the wrong senses. Some key figures in ancient Athens meet for a meal and a piss-up. Food, wine, sex and bodily functions – urinating, breaking wind and defecating (to use their polite forms for a moment) – are par for the course. And the reader will find a reasonable amount of such activities, or at least references to them, in the stories that follow. What was good enough for Plato is good enough for me. It's not merely a case of Australian vulgarity or the relaxed way in which we were brought up concerning these matters: there is a little-known but deeper continuity between Plato and Australia that shows up here.

Back to the *Symposium*. Agathon, the playwright, has just won the award for tragedy (his work does not survive), and he invites a few people the following evening for a meal: Eryximachus, the doctor; Phaedrus, a literary type; Pausanias, Agathon's lover; the comedian Aristophanes;

Socrates and his young friend Aristodemus. Alcibiades, who was to lead Athens to take up the disastrous Sicilian expedition that eventually lost them the Peloponnesian war, arrives later, totally drunk, to offer a paean to Socrates. They eat, reclining at table, agree not to drink too much so they can hold forth reasonably coherently (and send away the flute girl and do not call on the prostitutes so they can focus on the task at hand). Finally, they give in to the alcohol when a drunken Alcibiades turns up. Socrates – who is of course never affected by wine – Alcibiades and Agathon stay awake until dawn, but the others fall into their drunken slumbers much earlier.

The topic? It is, famously, love. Here we find the famous Diotima; or rather, she appears as someone Socrates met and whose wise words he passes on. And for Diotima, love is not merely the fleshly satisfaction of desires, of the need to procreate, nor even a higher spiritual relationship that can take place only between men. The highest form is, of course, the lover of wisdom, the philosopher, who reaches beyond the physical plane and achieves truth.

I am not so much interested in the content of *The Symposium* – there are simply too many little books on love about these days – but in the form. The event is a drinking party, and the scene is set up rather easily with an invitation to Socrates to attend. Or rather, Plato sets the scene up through the eyes of the youthful Aristodemus who is invited along by Socrates. Plato has them sit at the table – they recline on their left – and he notes various comments on the rituals of eating, but the point is to get to the discussion. In terms of getting across philosophical ideas, Plato keeps it brief. But it is in the interchange of dialogue that the ideas get aired, questioned and refined. The dialogue form of the *Symposium* is of course

ABBREVIATIONS

DH: Julius Wellhausen, *The Deuteronomistic History*. Trans J. Doull *et. al.* JSOTSup, 15; Sheffield: Sheffield Academic Press, 1991.

G: Hermann Gunkel, *Genesis*. Trans. Mark E. Biddle. Foreword by Ernest W. Nicholson. Macon, GA: Mercer University Press, 1997.

HB: Norman Gottwald, *The Hebrew Bible in its Social World and Ours*. Semeia Studies; Atlanta, GA: Scholars Press, 1993.

IP: Hermann Gunkel, *Introduction to the Psalms: The Genres of the Religious Lyric of Israel*. Completed by Joachim Begrich. Trans. James D. Nogalski. Macon, GA: Mercer University Press, 1998.

P: Julius Wellhausen, *Prolegomena to the History of Israel, with a Reprint of the Article 'Israel' from the Encyclopaedia Britannica*. Preface by W. Robertson Smith. Foreword to the Scholars Press Edition by Douglas A. Knight. Atlanta, GA: Scholars Press, 1994. Reprint of the 1885 edition.

PMB: Bible and Culture Collective, *The Postmodern Bible*. New Haven, CT: Yale University Press, 1995.

TTY: Norman Gottwald, 'Political Activism and Biblical Scholarship: An Interview'. Interviewed by Roland Boer. In Roland Boer (ed.). *Tracking 'The Tribes of Yahweh': On the Trail of a Classic*. JSOTSup, 351; London: Sheffield Academic Press, 2002, pp. 157-71.

TY: Norman Gottwald, *The Tribes of Yahweh: A Sociology of Liberated Israel 1050-1250*. Reprint Sheffield: Sheffield Academic Press, 1999. Original Maryknoll: Orbis, 1979.

Chapter 1

CAUGHT IN THE PROLEGOMENA:
JULIUS WELLHAUSEN AND SOURCE CRITICISM

"Gott in Himmel!" Julius cried. He had blocked for a few minutes the repeated knocking at his door. But he could ignore it no longer. Rueing the interruption to his writing, he put down his quill and walked stiffly to the worn front door, ducked slightly in the doorway and peered down at a compact young man with thick dark wavy hair and a beard around the edge of his round face. He was covered with the grime of travel. He said not a word of greeting.

The man in question almost broke his neck looking up at this solid German. A strong nose, piercing blue eyes, slightly balding blond hair and a full beard with tinges of grey greeted him. Wellhausen's clothes were old and comfortable – writer's garments, thought the man.

He introduced himself: "William Robertson Smith – our letters have crossed the English channel more times than I care to remember. Apologies for the surprise visit, but I had to talk with you. I'm at something of a loose end, heretic and jobless."

"Willkommen," Julius said with some hesitation, still utterly surprised by this nocturnal visitor from across the channel. He wondered at how they understood each other so well, Will with his Scots English and he himself with his German. Some new Pentecost, perhaps? It didn't matter; he suspended his disbelief and invited Will inside.

"Ja, I remember," he said, leaving Will standing on the pavement for a moment as something else pushed its way to the surface of his mind – whisky! The Scots are famous for whisky! Perhaps he has brought some with him. And I have been dying to smoke one or two of those wonderful White Owl cigars.

"Come in," he said, much more warmly now. "Come *in*!" Their greeting extended to a handshake, but such intimacy was a struggle. None of the Latin proclivity for elaborate hugs and kisses – it was just too much like the

Heimlich manoeuvre. Julius relieved Will of his travel-stained coat and small bag.

"Is this all you have brought?" he asked.

"I travel light."

Julius beckoned to the best chair in the house, ornate and plush. "Sit down; some food?"

"Oh *yes*," Will said, finding a position that avoided most of the pressure points and developing bedsores from the hard-seated trains, boats and carriages from Scotland. But there was one massive pimple right on the pressure point of his left buttock and it irritated the hell out of him. It was all he could do to resist from dropping his pants, propping his leg on the chair and squeezing the damn thing.

Julius opened the curtain of the sitting room window, lit some lamps in order to show off the room to neighbours taking a stroll in the early evening, and burrowed his way to the kitchen in the back of the house.

"William Robertson Smith has arrived from Scotland," he said to Marie, "do we have any food for him?"

"William who?" she said, sucking on an ancient, curling pipe while she sat contemplating the fire. "Never mind, there's some cold mutton under the cloth on the bench." Julius dug out a knife and hacked off a few rough pieces of dead sheep, then dropped them onto a plate and bore it out to the living room. He would have liked to kiss her, but the pipe was in the way, or perhaps groped her sensuous buttock, but *it* was enjoying the peasant's chair on which she sat.

Back in the living room, Will devoured the mutton as though it were a communion sacrifice. "Ah, that's good," he said through his last mouthful, and stretched out weary legs.

The moment Julius had been waiting for arrived – "Whisky?" he queried.

"Cigar?" Will asked.

Silently one drew out of his bag a half-full bottle of pure malt whisky while the other opened a drawer of his desk and retrieved two magnificent White Owl cigars. Will poured, Julius guillotined. Taper to cigar, they savoured the first mouthful of smoke, rolling it around until the sensitive buds in their mouths began to absorb the nicotine and tar. They exhaled simultaneously with the satisfaction that only a drug can induce.

After a sip of whisky to fire up the tastebuds, Julius asked, "Germany?"

"I am of course a heretic now, by the official word of the Free Kirk of Scotland, and all for teaching and promulgating your work and that of Graf. I'm out of a job and out of the Kirk, but it was a glorious trial. Daily, for months on end, the newspapers carried the story of the trial on their front pages. Even the English were entranced with what was happening in Scotland, and that's saying something. I was convicted, of course, but a large number of ministers of the Word and Sacrament put their names to a statement supporting the 'German scepticism.'"

"I did get wind of it over here," Julius said. "In fact, I have resigned from the Faculty of Theology at Tübingen and taken up a position with Arabic studies. Just didn't feel that my work was quite the right thing for students of theology."

Will frowned, disconcerted by the revelation. Through a tight mouth he said, "But I have just argued, in the preface to the English translation of your work, that 'the reader will learn how close are the bonds that connect the critical study of the Old Testament with the deepest and unchanging problems of living faith' (P: x). The Kirk is the natural home for your work and that of other critical scholars. What the hell did you leave *that* environment for?"

With that Will delved into his bag and brought out a well-worn copy of the English translation of the *Prolegomena*, stained in so many places with the oil from his fingers, corners turned over throughout in a way that Julius, with his respect for the written word, found slightly troubling. At least the spine isn't broken, he thought, but then checked himself as the pages came away from the cover. Will re-inserted them.

Will stood up, his voice taking on the liturgical lilt and rhythm of a minister of the Kirk before his congregation: "Of course, we have all read, and all do read the *Prolegomena*. We read it every day, transparently, in the dramas and dreams of our historical reconstructions, in its disputes and conflicts, in the defeats and victories of the various positions. But some day it is essential to read the *Prolegomena* to the letter. To read the text itself, complete, line by line, to return ten times to the first chapters, or the five schemes of the history of worship (place, sacrifice, feasts, priests and Levites, and endowment of the clergy), before coming down from the arid tablelands and plateaus of Part One into the promised land of texts, sources and history itself."

What a dummkopf, thought Julius, in fact, what an outright prick, although he allowed himself to say, "That's a little bombastic, Will."

Will broke off, remembering where he was, which was certainly not the pulpit nor even the heresy trial that had become so much a part of his life over the last few months. And the cigar and whisky in each hand were hardly fitting for the imagined scene – although how he had wished for a whisky at the countless difficult turns of the trial! 'Well,' he admitted as he sat down again, feeling asinine, "I'm not sure what came over me. I felt as though another voice had taken control of my mouth, very much like the prophets."

"Ohhhh, the prophets!" Julius cried in ecstasy, or at least what came close to it. *Now* Will had Julius' Lutheran-saturated attention.

"But it's true," continued Will after another mouthful of delicate smoke and countless carcinogenic chemicals, "that already everyone, at least in biblical studies, knows of your text, but few have in fact read it. As one person commented to me recently, why would you bother reading Wellhausen's lengthy book when there is any number of good summaries of it? And yet we do 'read' the Prolegomena in almost every essay or book, every debate and position taken in studies of the Hebrew Bible (a mere mention of source, or of JEP or P will do the trick). Yet, few of us have read and re-read the book itself, line by line. So let's have another look," Will suggested.

Julius remained silent. He stretched out his fingers, turned his hand over and looked long and hard at his fingernails, resisting the urge to scratch an itchy varicose vein in his leg. I must find some other way to write, he thought, since those damned veins keep popping out day after day standing at that desk.

Will took his silence as affirmation rather than, say, embarrassment. So he stripped off and plunged, so to speak, into the vast lake of Wellhausen's text, the chill of its alpine waters drawing a gasp and a curse. "What I see," began Will in a rush of logorrhoea, "is a deep hatred for priests and historical falsification, a tendency for your grasp on historical safety to touch on the all too slippery rock of the biblical text, a romanticist's passion for nature and spontaneity, and a *real* liking for gore."

Julius's ears rang. This was hardly what he expected. What in the world is he talking about? He paused, sipped some whisky and replied, slowly and just a little stiffly, "Well... it's true that I have a profound love for fresh earth, for a human naïveté that joyfully and spontaneously celebrates nature and agricultural cycles. Anything that cuts the trunk of such a life, that ring-barks the natural and spur-of-the-moment expression of human passion and sacredness should be chased from the field, uncovered in whatever way possible and exposed as inauthentic and fundamentally false. It is, you know, the opposition of life over death. What is earlier and more natural breathes and expresses life – and is thereby *more* historically reliable – while what comes later is leaden, a deadly weight that suffocates and drowns."

But Will was on a roll, and Julius let him have his head.

"Your general argument is reasonably well known," continued Will, "or at least *part* of it is. Building on the work of Graf, you argue that the Pentateuch comprises four sources – the Yahwist, Elohist, Deuteronomist and Priestly writers and editors, along with the proposed locations and dates. Thus in the earliest text, the Yahwist's coming from the tenth century BCE [sc BCE throughout] and the south, we find a wonderful storyteller, God is in close relationship with human beings, and religious commitment is a spontaneous thing; the Elohist, who comes from the eighth century BCE from the northern kingdom of Israel has God retreat into the heavens somewhat, behind the veils of mystery and distance, and our walk on earth becomes a little darker; the Deuteronomic source from the seventh century BCE operates with the stark doctrine of divine retribution for good or evil deeds; and the Priestly writer, the last one coming from the fifth century BCE (that is, after the return from the exile to Babylon in 538 BCE) is concerned with order, worship, the cult and the right way to appease God. These priests have edited all of the above and put their stamp on it."

"Not quite!" broke in Julius. "Oh God, I'm sick of these misreadings! This mantra – you know JEDP – does little justice to my argument concerning the Hexateuch. When I do talk about it in that all important eighth chapter, I contrast the combined document of JE with P. I hardly mention the separate sources J and E, and I pass lightly over D."

"I'll give you that one," Will said, "but you aren't entirely blameless, for you sharpen your wordsmith's tools in those extraordinary summaries with which you close out chapters. And it's these summaries that draw the eye of harried teachers of biblical studies and equally pressed writers of introductions to the Hebrew Bible." Will opened a well-worn page that he had read to students and church dignitaries on countless occasions:

"The second Jehovistic source, E, breathes the air of the prophets much more markedly, and shows a more advanced and thorough-going religiosity... The Deity appears less primitive than in J, and does not approach men in bodily form, but calls to them from heaven, or appears to them in dreams. The religious element has become more refined, but at the same time more energetic, and has laid hold even of elements heterogeneous to itself, producing on occasion such strange mixtures as that in Gen. xxxi. 10-13. Then the law comes in and leavens the Jehovistic narrative, first the Deuteronomic (in Genesis even, and then quite strongly in Exodus and Joshua), while last of all, in the Priestly Code, under the influence of the legislation of the post-exilic restoration, there is brought about a complete metamorphosis of the old tradition. The law is the key to the understanding even of the Priestly Code. All the distinctive peculiarities of the work are connected with the influence of the law: everywhere we hear the voice of theory, rule, judgment.

> What was said above of the cultus may be repeated word for word of the legend: in the early time it may be likened to the green tree which grows out of the ground as it will and can; at a later time it is dry wood that is cut and made to a pattern with compass and square"

Julius' fingers began stroking the wood of his armrest, the sensuous feel of the grain as erotic as the skin of a lover. Who cannot but want to water the live tree, he thought, to ensure its survival rather than its death?

"You miss the point!" he cried. "This apparent summary of the documentary hypothesis is in fact a brief example of what I call 'source-sifting' (P: 360), tracing the inner development of the tradition through its intermediate stages all the way from J to P – but it is something I do not do most of the time!"

Before this thundering German (no wonder they use so many capitals!), Will wished he were the stuffing in his seat. At least we Scots hold in our anger...sometimes.

"In fact," continued Julius, "I was actually giving weight and substance to Graf's hypothesis, since I'm largely concerned with the relationship between JE and P. Here," he said, grabbing the book from Will, "let me plagiarize myself." He stood to quote from his text (imagine him reading with a thick German accent; well, actually, he was reading in German, but we'll have to content ourselves with the accent):

> "I differ from Graf chiefly in this, that I always go back to the centralisation of the cultus, and deduce from it the particular divergences. My whole position is contained in my first chapter: there I have placed in a clear light that which is of such importance for Israelite history, namely, the part taken by the prophetical party in the great metamorphosis of the worship, which by no means came about of itself. Again I attach much more weight than Graf did to the change of ruling ideas which runs parallel with the change in the institutions and usages of worship; this has been shown mostly in the second part of the present work. Almost more important to me than the phenomena themselves, are the presuppositions which lie behind them" (P: 368).

"And we argue," Julius continued, "controversially no doubt, that the Priestly material could hardly be the first or oldest source, but *must* be the last, since the priests' heavy hand ranges far and wide over the texts."

At the mention of priests, the Wee Free in Will erupted, his Presbyterian dislike of anything priestly joining the flow of Julius' words. "*Priests,*" he yelled, "suck the life out of any religious worship. All they're worried about are the minutiae of correct observance, the stipulation of how even the smallest acts are to be performed. They are concerned only with their own power, with temporal and not heavenly concerns, so much so that they will even falsify history to achieve these ends."

"Ja, I *hate* the priests." The venom of his words threatened to splatter itself over the book that sat open in his lap. "They are conniving, self-centred, petty and greedy manipulators of people and history. The Priestly Code 'could only gain an entrance when the legend had died away from the memory and the heart of the people, and was dead at the root' (P: 362)."

Julius' cigar had died in the excitement; he reached across to the fire and drew out a burning stick to relight it.

Will took advantage of the pause. "The problem," he said, "is that we have actually given too much ground to your critics and disciples (of which I must confess I am one). So often they see your contribution precisely in debates over the source hypothesis of the Hexateuch. It may be the sharpest example of your hypothesis, but it also neglects the extent of your argument. You also deal at length with Chronicles and then Judges, Samuel and Kings – in that *reverse* order to boot, in order to show how the priestly touch is both pervasive and late on the Hebrew Bible. All of this, however – Chronicles, Judges, Samuel and Kings, and then the Hexateuch – comes in the second and middle section of the book. But what *I'm* interested in are the first and last sections of the book. The *first* part concerns itself of all things with the place of worship, sacrifice, sacred feasts, the distinction between priests and Levites, and the payment or endowment of the clergy. The *last* section opens out to the broad issues of law, oral and written torah and theocracy, or really hierocracy. And in both you obsess about the priests."

In fact, Julius couldn't get them out of his head. He recalled writing the book, how the priests crowded his thoughts by day when he wrote and by night his dreams teamed with vestments, incense and ritual. Even now, they were still the stuff of his nightmares. "Why can't I get rid of them?" he asked himself aloud. "If I try to exclude them, they are there all the more strongly, grinning and teasing me, and if I indulge in them, let them have free reign, they love it. All of my shouting and cursing simply makes no difference. Why do I hate them and love them, obsess about them and dismiss them? Why do I eat and evacuate plates full of all things priestly?"

It was Will's turn to be astounded. Was this the great Julius Wellhausen? he asked himself. Is he perhaps an obsessional neurotic? But then a perverse corner of his psyche kicked in and he threw himself into Julius' seductive prose on all fours.

"Surely," he said, leaning forward to poke the fire and throw on another piece of timber, "your hand must have tired of writing 'Priestly Code' on page after page, for in your eyes it is the bane of the Hebrew Bible, setting the agenda for that all-pervasive final editing of the Pentateuch and the very possibility of Chronicles. And those responsible for the Priestly Code, the coterie of priests sequestered away in that first ivory tower, are a somewhat grotesque bunch – senile, unimaginative, dogmatic and opinionated, indeed rude, crude, mechanical, ascetic, cancerous and parasitic."

"Ja! Ja!" Julius jumped up from his chair, remembering the words that flowed from his own quill. He held up the book and cried: "Thus, on the instructions to boil or bake the manna in the desert" – he flipped a few pages – " 'Nor is it any sign of originality, rather of senility, that in the Priestly Code the manna is not eaten raw, but boiled and baked' (P: 353)." He turned to another page: "The sabbath ceases to be 'the joyous breathing-time from the load of life which a festival affords' and becomes an 'ascetic exercise' that sucks the life out of the celebration of rest (P: 115). And again," he said, peering at yet another leaf, "over against the close connection between domestic and foreign events that we find in Samuel-Kings, the priest-saturated text of Chronicles tears them apart in a 'rude and mechanical manner' (P: 178). Genesis too falls under the sway of these morose and scuttling individuals, who have simply not seen enough light of day in their little writing dens. For all its profound influence, Genesis 1 is a feeble attempt at pseudo-scientific explanation, shorn of the wild growth of myth or legend. Characterized by a 'pale colour' it merely postulates chaos and 'all that follows is reflection, systematic construction; we can easily follow the calculation from point to point' (P: 298). But even in Judges, where the touch is lighter and more characteristic of the Deuteronomistic revision, we find the tedium of priestly concerns. In that well-known rhythm of obedience, backsliding and rescue, I find evidence of the baleful religious connection between events: 'One is reminded of the "Satz," "Gegensatz," and "Vermittlung" of the Hegelian philosophy when one's ear has been caught by the monotonous beat with which the history here advances, or rather moves in a circle. Rebellion, affliction, conversion, peace; rebellion, affliction, conversion, peace' (P: 231). And then there is the famous wooden notion of immediate divine retribution in Chronicles, in which there is an astonishing correspondence between obedience and blessing, and conversely between disobedience and punishment – instantly, without delay or mitigation: 'Never does sin miss its punishment, and never where misfortune occurs is guilt wanting' (P: 203)."

In his haste to find further pages of priestly conniving, the tome slipped from his grasp and crushed a toe on its way to the floor. While Julius desperately sought relief from his excruciating toe in some more whisky, Will picked the book up and charged on.

"Sometimes," he said, "sarcasm creeps in from its quiet place by the door, leaping lightly upon the manuscript. For instance, in your drive to prove Graf's hypothesis that the Priestly revision is last rather than first, you write: 'But the suddenness with which this full-grown hierocracy descended on the wilderness from the skies is only matched by the suddenness with which it afterward disappeared in Canaan, leaving no trace behind it' (P: 127). But my favourite would have to be the narrative of the flood, in which P is woven so tightly around JE that the strands are difficult to untangle. In the midst of the flood to end all floods, Noah becomes the priestly mariner: 'When the water is at its height, on the seventeenth of the second month, the flood is fifteen cubits above the highest mountains – Noah having apparently not forgotten, in spite of his anxiety, to heave the lead and to mark the date in his log-book' (P: 310). Suddenly, the narrative loses its charm – 'All that is idyllic and naïve is consistently stripped off the legend as far as possible' (P: 310)."

Julius choked over his own mirth, while Will just let it rip before downing another Scotch. They had both loosened up, hunkered down by the fire, and were ready to talk and laugh long into the night.

"The problem," said Will when he had stopped laughing, "is that if the Priestly revision is the last in line, its presence is pervasive, running all over the text, setting its dominant tone and theological agenda. So much so that it determines 'modern' discussions of the Hebrew Bible. It becomes normative, and any other material must fit into this schema (see P: 52). Apart from the obvious point you make here, there is also the awareness that the biblical text in some inexplicable manner sets the agenda for its own interpretation."

"Yet," continued Will, "this is hardly a benign process, innocent perhaps apart from a few priestly predilections. Criminal would be a more apt term, if not sinful, except that you steer clear of such theological terms. And it's not merely disdain that underwrites your discussion. You have a bodily loathing for priestly things: 'a monstrous growth' (P: 342) is how you describe the legislative material that swamps the Pentateuch from Exodus onwards. Cancerous, those priests and their writing. Or it could be a foreign body that invades your organs and grows inside its host: 'the legal forces its way into the narrative, and once there spreads itself and takes up more and more room' (P: 342)." Had he the requisite filmic experience, Will would no doubt have proffered the analogy of the grotesque parasite in Ridley Scott's *Alien*. "Otherwise the parasite entwines itself around the outside of the tree, squeezing the sap out of its source of nourishment like a strangler fig or ivy."

By now Julius was squirming, trying to poke from his mind's eye the image of cancerous growths and parasites growing within their hosts. The Scots are a strange race, he thought. But Will read to him his own words:

> "In the Jehovistic history-book Genesis is a most important part, and occupies at least half of the whole work: in the Priestly Code, Genesis quite disappears in comparison with the later books. Only with the Mosaic legislation does this work arrive at its own ground, and it at once stifles the narrative under a mass of legislative matter. Here also there is a thin historical thread running parallel to the Jehovist, but we constantly lose sight of it from the repeated interruptions made by extensive ritual laws and statistical statements" (P: 342). [end of indent]

"Well then," Will said, "all this venom. Where does it come from?" He answered his own question: "From that mighty stream of Enlightenment anti-clericalism, or maybe the Protestant abhorrence of all things papist. No small matter this, since in my childhood we were subjected to our daily bout of anti-papist sentiment at the hands of my Calvinist father. But there's a deeper current that sustains the ones closer to the surface, and that's the curious legacy of Romanticism – in your country it's been particularly strong. But Romanticism, Julius, is *so* ambivalent: it's all about nature and spontaneity, but it's also one of the sources of anti-Semitism."

"Anti-Semitism?" retorted a surprised and offended Julius. "You can't be serious!"

"Afraid so, old man."

"Where?"

"What about this? 'The whole question ultimately resolves itself into that of historical credibility; and to what conclusions this leads we have already seen. The alterations and additions of Chronicles are all traceable to the same fountain-head – the Judaising of the past, in which otherwise the people of that day would have been unable to recognise their ideal' (P: 223). Or: 'It is not the case that the Jews had any profound respect for their ancient history' (P: 161)."

"But I'm talking about the priests responsible for Chronicles here," Julius said. "What's anti-Semitic about that?"

"How about the phrase 'Judaising of the past'? And then there is this: 'The whole section 1 Chron. xxii.–xxix. is a startling instance of that statistical phantasy of the Jews which revels in vast sums of money on paper (xxii. 14), in artificial marshalling of names and numbers (xxiii.–xxvii.), in the enumeration of mere subjects without predicates, which simply stand on parade and neither signify nor do anything. The monotony is occasionally broken only by unctuous phrases, but without refreshing the reader. Let the experiment of reading the chapters through be tried' (P: 181). Later on you return to this 'Jewish fancy, a fancy which, it is well known, does not design nor sketch, but counts and constructs, and produces nothing more than barren plans' (P: 348).''

"No, *no*!" protested Julius, "you've misunderstood me! 'Judaism' and 'Jewish' are *historical* terms, designating the people that came back from the Babylonian Exile. They lived in the province of Yehud; they first became known as Jews then. These are the characters I mean – and they're the *same* priestly authors of Chronicles, *and* those responsible for the Priestly code and the final revision of the Hexateuch."

"It's a little difficult to see the difference," responded Will. "Far too often it feels as though you're writing about contemporary Jews, as though nothing much has in fact changed. But then you can't escape a sentence such as this: 'It is well known that there have never been more audacious history-makers than the Rabbis, but Chronicles accords evidence sufficient that this evil propensity goes back to a very early time' (P: 161). Here's the connection, the continuity from Chronicles to the medieval Rabbis."

By now Julius was silent, seeing for the first time, with great dismay, how strong it really was in his work.

Will went on. "Now I will grant you this, that you dislike Roman Catholics as much as Jews – all because they're priests. But you can't get out of it so easily, for isn't Midrash a distinctly Jewish practice?"

"True," Julius said slowly, sensing where this was heading.

"So how do you explain a passage like this, where you discuss 2 Chronicles 24.27 and 2 Chronicles 13.22?

> "Midrash is the consequence of the conservation of all the relics of antiquity, a wholly peculiar artificial reawakening of dry bones, especially by literary means, as is shown in the preference for lists of names and numbers. Like ivy it overspreads the dead trunk with extraneous life, blending old and new in a strange combination. It is a high estimate of tradition that leads to its being thus modernised; but in the process it is twisted and perverted, and set off with foreign accretions in the most arbitrary way" (P: 227).

"Isn't it an inescapable conclusion?" But by now Julius' responses were somewhat uncertain.

"Well no, actually," replied Will. "You can have a go at the priests all you like – even if it's an obsession of yours – but there's no necessary connection with the Jews. In *some* cases your comments are just unnecessary asides that show your prejudices all the more clearly."

Deeply troubled, Julius said, "I need to go to the can," and raced out to the back of the house. Sitting over that cold metal drum in the freezing toilet, he pondered Will's words as he squeezed and pushed to no avail. The knot remained locked in his anus. Lots of antis, he reflected – anti-Semitism, anti-clericalism, anti-papism, the only exception is Romanticism. If only I could find some anti-constipation material! I've tried everything, from cod-liver oil to eating beans, and nothing works. "Oh how I wish I could have a *decent crap*!" he shouted into the darkness, setting off a chorus of neighbourhood dogs.

Back in the sitting room, decidedly unrelieved, he located another couple of cigars and offered a thankful Will another one. The whisky, however, was a different matter, for Will had downed the last of the bottle in Julius' absence. Strange how clearly we think and speak after so much whisky at this late hour, he pondered.

Julius looked around. "All I have is some cane spirit," he said somewhat sheepishly.

"Cane spirit?"

"From a strange fellow in Australia, of all places. They dare not call it rum. Careful with that *flame*! It might catch fire. And it's good for dealing with rodents: it burns out their guts."

"Perfect," Will said.

So Julius removed a few books in the commentary series from Keil and Delitzsch from one of the shelves and retrieved the fire water. The bottle top was in the shape of an armoured helmet – like nothing either of them had seen before. Cylindrical, it had a rough rectangle cut out for the eyes.

"Ned Kelly?" queried Will as he read the words on the bottle.

"What they call a 'bushranger' – quite a folk hero in Australia who kept the police on the run. Eventually they shot out his legs and hung him: nothing like a martyr for the fight against oppression."

Will was intrigued until he tasted the first drop. It *burned*! If there was a threat of impending sleep, it was well and truly gone by now.

Jolted by the cane spirit, he resumed: "Not only can't you stand the priests as priests, but it's what they do with history that's their greatest sin. They *falsify* history, playing loose with the tradition, freely rewriting it as seems best to them. And the reason? They impose on that history the theological categories of theocracy, which is really just hierocracy, their own rule."

"Chronicles is the worst," picked up Julius, "a creation out of whole cloth by conniving priests." By now Julius had drunk enough to quote himself endlessly. " 'One might as well try to hear the grass growing as attempt to derive from such a source as this a historical knowledge of the conditions of ancient Israel' (P: 215)."

Will had always had a tendency to take metaphors at face value – a genetic mutation perhaps, or a curious feature of Scottish culture. And so his mind locked onto the image of Wellhausen lying on the ground in one of Tübingen's university gardens, one ear to the ground and a copy of the Hebrew Bible open at Chronicles. Knowing he shouldn't, Will drew back on the cigar. The smoke ripped the back off his throat, so he tossed down another mouthful of cane spirit, hoping it would counteract the effect of the smoke. A poor assumption, he soon realized.

"I'm intrigued," Will said, when he had coughed enough to return his throat to a moderate level of contamination, "for in the Hexateuch and in Samuel–Kings you *do* find sources, agreeing with Graf for the layering and revision of the traditions. But with Chronicles you deny any sources. The only text with which that author or those authors were working was Samuel–Kings itself. Isn't there a contradiction here in your method?"

"The problem," replied Julius, "is that Chronicles is the culminating moment of the Priestly revision and final editing of the Hebrew Bible. If they consistently reworked the older sources in the Hexateuch and Samuel–Kings, by Chronicles they had run out of materials and set out to write their own version of the history. So in Chronicles the priests finally got to do what they always wanted to do – write the history in their way. But it's hardly *history* anymore – it's pure fabrication for the sake of some worthless theological ideas."

Will came back at him. "But what about those biblical critics who argue that Chronicles itself works with older sources apart from Samuel–Kings, and that these sources are quite ancient and potentially reliable?"

"Theologically motivated *morons!*" blurted Julius. "As if any attack on the reliability of the Bible is an attack on religion itself. They seem to think – the morons – that the unreliability of the Bible is homologous to the untrustworthiness of God. You'd think De Wette had laid that one to rest, but no, they keep on trying."

Will had been flicking pages while Julius spoke. After a pause on one page he found the passage for which he was looking, although he had to focus somewhat harder as there seemed to be two pages before him: " 'But since that date [De Wette in 1826] many a theological Sisyphus has toiled to roll the stone again wholly or half-way up the hill…with peculiar results' (P: 222)."

Will continued. "I've gotta agree with De Wette and you on this count: Chronicles is pure invention; there are no ancient sources behind it."

"One example," Julius said, "the genealogies: here we have a really banal creativity. As you know, the priests love their genealogies. Peppered throughout the Hexateuch where possible, the Chronicler finally takes flight with the first chapters of Chronicles. It is a strange mindset, one that attempts to 'give a genealogical expression to all connections and associations of human society whatsoever, to create artificial families on all hands and bring them into blood relationship' (P: 211). You can see how it happens: he has a few bits and pieces, material comes to hand, looks like it may be a beginning and an end and the bridge is soon completed. It is 'as if the whole of public life resolved itself into a matter of cousinship' (P: 211). Only a period of political stagnation can produce such an incestuous idea of the nation, and only a mind that cares not a jot or a tittle for history could reorganize families, create bloodlines and let his imagination run."

"But no matter how much you hate it, you do read Chronicles," retorted Will, "in great painstaking detail."

"Ja…that is true." The images that he constantly tried to banish from his mind came crowding in – the extraordinarily sensual women priests in tight garments, all valleys and peaks, and the muscle-bound men, angular and strong beneath the priestly robes. Not having read Freud he could barely make sense of these fantasies in terms of the erotics of knowledge. All he could do was return to the priestly texts and fantasize concerning what lust was repressed by the obsessive concern with ritual, dress, interior decoration, music and song, and the minutiae of correct observance. His wife had urged him so often to don priestly garb before and during sex: the thought both excited and repulsed him. Freud would have told him that disgust is so often the incitement to desire.

A question had been teasing Will's mind for some time now, but every time he turned to catch it, it scampered off into a hidden corner and he lost it again.

Instead he said: "Let's put the question of reliability in a basket for the moment. You take another tack in your effort to date the sources themselves. That is, the sources themselves speak of history obliquely, like a sideways glance. In other words, it's not what the sources say but their context that's important. That's a real breakthrough, Julius!"

"But of course," Julius said. "While Chronicles and the Priestly source reflect the context of Persian imperial control – how else could you have futile dreams of a theocracy? – the Jehovist comes from a much earlier world."

"Even here you like the Jehovist better," Will said.

"Who wouldn't?" Julius replied. And, since he was *really* enjoying quoting himself in a self-serving kind of way, he rolled on – just as he tended to do in the book:

> "In the Jehovist the present everywhere shines through, he in no way conceals his own age; we are told that Babylon is the great world-city, that the Assyrian Empire is in existence, with the cities of Nineveh (!) and Calah and Resen; that the Canaanites had once dwelt in Palestine, but had long been absorbed by the Israelites. The writer of the Priestly Code is very careful not to do anything like this. He brushes up the legend and makes history of it according to the rules of art; he kills it as legend, and deprives it of all real value, such as it possesses, not indeed for the history of primitive times, but for that of the age of the kings" (P: 338).

"So the Jehovist makes it easy for us and the Priestly writer tries to cover his tracks?"

"Pretty much," Julius said. "But it's precisely because he cuts out contemporary allusions that we know he's not writing at the same time or earlier than the Jehovist. Conniving bugger, but I've uncovered his fraud!"

"You go *much* further than that," Will said, "for you begin with a historical reconstruction and then place the sources within that history. What I mean is that famous analysis of the history of worship with which you begin the book. You write, 'After laboriously collecting the data offered by the historical and prophetical books, we constructed a sketch of the Israelite history of worship; we then compared the Pentateuch with this sketch, and recognised that one element of the Pentateuch bore a definite relation to this phase of the history of worship, and another element of the Pentateuch to that phase of it' (P: 367)."

Julius felt a glow of admiration for the Scot, for he had identified the essence of his own argument: *the history of the texts was intimately tied up with the history behind them.* But Will had paused, looking entirely unconvinced. Julius nervously scratched his neck, wondering whether bed was a good idea.

Finally, Will spoke: "But how do you reconstruct that history, Julius?"

"From the texts, of course," Julius said, with a residue of confidence.

"That means you need reliable texts themselves and not just hypotheses concerning their historical contexts."

"*Yes...*"

"Well then," Will said, warming up, "let's go back to the difference between Samuel–Kings and Chronicles. Why is the former so different from the latter?"

"Samuel–Kings," replied Julius, "is the historical foil for Chronicles' fancy. The unforgivable fabrication of Chronicles, all for the sake of some theological ideal, is simply not found in Samuel–Kings, which is a rich, all too human, narrative: 'What a length of time these affairs demand, how natural is their development, how many human elements mingle in their course – cunning, and treachery, and battle, and murder!' (P: 173). The contrast with Chronicles couldn't be greater: 'all in Chronicles that is not derived from Samuel and Kings, has a uniform character not only in substance, but also in its awkward and frequently unintelligible language – plainly belonging to a time in which Hebrew was approaching extinction – in its artificiality of style, deriving its vitality exclusively from biblical reminiscences' (P: 210-11)."

Now the question was beginning to rise from the murky depths of Will's mind. Heresy, travel, cigars and cane spirit – not a good mix when we are burning the midnight oil, he thought to himself.

"A stark contrast!" he said to Julius.

"Ja, indeed."

"But hold on!" Will cried. "Haven't Judges, Samuel and Kings also suffered from the priestly bane. 'The discolouring influences begin early,' (P: 293) you write: 'What in the common view appears to be the specific character of Israelite history, and has chiefly led to its being called *sacred* history, rests for the most part on a later re-painting of the original picture' (P: 293)."

"You try as hard as you can," continued Will, "to distinguish Chronicles from Judges, Samuel and Kings. *But* isn't the final editing of Judges, Samuel and Kings done by the Deuteronomist, and that's pretty priestly. Isn't Deuteronomy in its original – Josianic – form 'a pure law-book' (P: 345). And the Law is of course central to the perspective of the priests. Different types of priests maybe, but they're still priests!"

"True," Julius said cautiously, a little worried where Will's argument was going. He did have a knack of finding priests everywhere. In fact there were so many under his bed there would have been no room for communists, and *they* were starting to cause a ruckus.

"And we do get in Judges to Kings and indeed in the Hexateuch," Will went on, "pieces of complete historical fabrication. For instance, on Abraham you write that he 'might with more likelihood be regarded as a free creation of unconscious art' (P: 320). My question is then whether the pure fancy of Chronicles may not also apply to Judges, Samuel and Kings, or indeed the Hexateuch itself, where the deadening hand of the Priestly Code – 'which contemplates a purely ideal Israel, with ideal boundaries, and leaves the sober reality so far out of sight' (P: 160) – is of one with Chronicles?"

Julius sat silently for a few moments, exhaled a dense plume of smoke and studied the fire intensely. "I could get used to this cane spirit," he said in avoidance of the question.

Still he paused, hoping Will might doze off. But the Scot's eyes were bright. He leaned forward in his chair. Julius finally gave in and said, "As far as the historical books are concerned, the less overtly theological it is, the more historically reliable it is. In fact, when the struggle of everyday human cause and effect is primary, then we have much more reliable historical material. 'History has to take account principally, if not exclusively, of the natural version, which is dry in tone and lets things speak for themselves, not overlaying the simple story with the significance of its consequences' (P: 244). The succession narrative of Solomon (2 Samuel 9–2 Kings 2) is probably the best example of all of this, along with 1 Samuel 14.52–2 Samuel 8.18 on David and Saul. Both are 'marked by an essentially historical character' (P: 262)."

"What about the Hexateuch, then?" pushed Will. "You've written that the Jehovistic work, as you call it 'was originally a pure history-book, so Deuteronomy, when it was first discovered, was a pure law-book' (P: 345)."

"The Jehovist is *earthy and lively*," Julius said. "He transmits legends in a way that reflects life and the people. He is not afraid of myth and marvel, like in the creation stories, nor of the legends of the patriarchs, who turn out to express many of the concerns and wishes of the individual Israelite. Yahweh walks and talks with the people; he's one of them writ large. The Jehovist's freshness and vitality make the text the earliest and most reliable. For instance, on the patriarchs:

> "Abraham, Isaac, and Jacob, are not mere names, but living forms, ideal prototypes of the true Israelite. They are all peace-loving shepherds, inclined to live quietly beside their tents, anxious to steer clear of strife and clamour, in no circumstances prepared to meet force with force and oppose injustice with the sword. Brave and manly they are not, but they are good fathers of families, a little under the dominion of their wives, who are endowed with more temper. They serve Jehovah in essentially the same way as their descendents in historical times; religion with them does not consist of sacrifice alone, but also of an upright conversation and trustful resignation to God's providence... The stories about him do not pretend to be moral, the feeling they betray is in fact that of undissembled joy in all the artifices and tricks of the patriarchal rogue" (P: 320).

"Myth, marvel, legend..." Will said. "But is it historically *reliable*?"

"Ah yes, but it is, because he gives unfettered expression to the legends and myths of the people, voices their hopes and fears, their celebrations and disappointments."

Will couldn't take much more: "But that's hardly the same thing as the very human sections of Judges, Joshua and Kings, where God is basically absent."

"Yes, it *is*," Julius fired back, "for both are clearly the earliest sources and therefore the most reliable. 'Only it may stand as a general principle, that the nearer history is to its origin the more profane it is' (P: 244). The priestly texts, especially Chronicles, are obviously late and so much out of touch with the time of the stories that they have no idea what was going on. Above all you can *feel* the vitality of these sources, sense the energy in them. The blood rushes through their veins, whereas the Priestly Code and Chronicles are more like the walking dead."

Will kept pushing him: "So whatever is earlier is better, historically speaking, although that shows up in different ways – human interaction, myth and legend. But *feeling*? One text feels more reliable, in terms of transmitting factual historical information, than another. Is that what it comes down to? Or, if I may quote you: 'To anyone who knows anything about history it is not necessary to prove…' (P: 150)."

"Well, of *course*!" replied Julius. "Isn't ancient history precisely that? We have a hunch or two, back them up with some critical arguments – the more human and earlier the better – and move on from there. Ancient history, you know, relies on very few pieces of data and then relies on your own critical imagination to link those few pieces together in a narrative that makes sense."

Will sat back for moment, marvelling at the way his weariness had fled the field long ago. Even his vision had returned. Apart from sex, he thought, there was nothing quite like a good argument to fire up body and mind, when your body forgot about fatigue, hunger and cold, until that curious moment when you finally break and think, hell, it's cold, or God, I'm hungry. It used to be like that with his father (the arguments, not the sex), for the two of them had gone at it like prize warriors for hours on end, and then come away thinking, damn, that was a good discussion.

So he launched into the next point: "Let's go back to that nagging question of the earliest material. So, we have two criteria for what might count as earliest, and therefore reliable – the profane and the lively, if I may put it in this way. But elsewhere you bring in other items, especially poetry and prophetic material."

"Ja, obviously poetry comes before prose in the same way that oral texts come before written ones. Let's take the example of Judges 4 and 5. The poetic text of Judges 5 is a very old text: it mentions only ten tribes, including Machir, of which only seven turn up for battle. Deborah is the hero and Barak her subordinate. Clearly, it's a text that celebrates an early victory over the Canaanites. Judges 4, by contrast, is much less reliable, obviously built on the poem but making Barak the chief-in-command and killing Sisera off with a tent peg."

"It's like *quicksand*!" thundered the Scot. "Now we have poetry as both early and reliable. But doesn't poetry play with language, deal in images? And as for the syntax – it often makes no sense whatsoever."

For a moment Julius pitied the congregations Will may have berated. All he could manage – meekly – was a quotation: " 'In the field of miracle, poetry is manifestly earlier than prose' (P: 244)."

"In the field of *miracle*!" Will exploded with an exasperated sigh, blowing ash all over Julius. "My *God*, man, if miracle, the field of poetry, is the earliest of all, then how in hell can it be reliable historically?"

Everything had seemed so certain to Julius when he wrote the book: the conniving priests who falsified history; the early text of the Jehovist, full of vitality; the profane chunks of Judges, Samuel and Kings; and the occasional gem of an early poem. But now all that was solid was beginning to melt into air – his certainty uncertainty, his confidence doubt.

But Will wouldn't let him go, pursuing him until he gave out his last, carefully hidden and dirty little secret. "The prophets?" he goaded.

Julius finally felt that ground firm up under his feet, his soles gaining a grip on the slippery terrain. "The *prophets*, oh yes, I mean the great writing prophets. In their case, 'the chief, or rather the only, weight is to be attached to their authentic testimony' (P: 47, note 1). Oh that Elijah had written something, anything, for he would have joined the others. Still, the accounts we have of him must have been drawn from the impression produced by a real character."

"*Why*" asked Will, "is their testimony so authentic?"

"Not only were they profoundly ethical," replied Julius, "the first proponents of that sublime ethical monotheism, but they were very much inspired, heard God speaking to them directly, 'theopneust' in fact, 'independent of all traditional and preconceived human opinions' (P: 48)."

As soon as he said it he knew he had crossed a line, staring wildly into territory he had not travelled for so long.

" 'God-breathed,' " whispered Will. " 'All scripture is inspired by God, and profitable for teaching, reproof, for correction, and for training in righteousness' it says in 2 Timothy 3:16. 'Theopneust' is a New Testament term: Scripture is Scripture because it is inspired by God. Man, *you are using a theological category*! Their work is reliable because *God spoke to them*!"

They both sat in silence, mouths open.

Will broke the silence, rising from his chair. "*Damn*, Julius," he said, "maybe that explains why you were never able to write volume two – the actual history itself for which this book is the prolegomena. All we had to be content with was that Britannica article. I hate to admit it, but it doesn't live up to your usual brilliance. It's a bit flat, not written with your usual passion."

"Why, what was wrong with it?" asked Julius, shifting in his seat and feeling the huge constipated knot at precisely that point where he should have felt most comfortable.

"Well all you do for the most part is rehash the biblical text, starting with Moses."

"True enough, but how else do you write a history of Israel? All we have in most cases is that text."

"Yes, and I know that you work so hard to identify the material that might be reliable historically, but so often it reads like an allegory. The biblical material becomes an allegory for the history of Israel, and if we know how to read the allegory we can know the history itself."

"That's not fair," Julius said sulkily.

Will dropped his small Scots behind in the chair, suddenly feeling somewhat giddy. "Let's take an example, your interpretation of the Jacob and Esau story. I'll start by quoting you:

> "The two boys grow up very different. Esau is a rough and sunburnt hunter, ranges about in the desert, and lives from day to day without care: Jacob, a pious, smooth man, stays at home beside the tents, and understands the value of things which his unsophisticated brother disregards. The former is the favourite of his father, the autochthonous Isaac, the latter is preferred by the mother, the Aramaean Rebecca; the former stays in his own land and takes his wives from the original population of south Canaan and the Sinaitic peninsula, the latter emigrates, and brings his wives from Mesopotamia. Thus the contrast is distinctly prefigured, which at a later time appeared, between the rough Edom, sprung from the soil and having his roots in it, and smoother, more civilised Israel, which had more affinity with the great powers of the world. By means of deceit and trickery the younger brother succeeds in depriving the elder of the paternal blessing and of the right of the first-born; the elder, in consequence of this, determines to kill him, and the situation becomes strained. Edom was a people and a kingdom before Israel,

but was then overshadowed by Israel, and even subjugated at last by David:' hence the fierce hatred between the brother-nations, of which Amos speaks" (P: 322).

"I *like* that section," Julius said; "it's the model for what I do in the Britannica article."

"Well, that's a shame," Will said in a moment of anticipatory criticism. "God, Julius, I can't tell whether it's allegory or history: Esau is rough and sprung from the soil, just like Edom, whereas Israel is smooth and sophisticated, knowing the better things of life, just like Jacob. In fact, I don't think you can actually write that history. *You* write, on Esau and Jacob, 'But this is not the place to trace the historical interpretation of the stories further' (P: 324). You *couldn't* write volume two of the proposed history, so when we were translating and publishing the *Prolegomena* we had to compromise with the translation and put the *Britannica* article in its place."

Julius was stung: here his greatest work was mercilessly being pulled to pieces by this damned Scot. Now he wished he had never let him in. He wouldn't be able to write for days. His throat hurt and his mind was spinning, and not just from the conversation.

"Haven't you anything nice to say at all?" he asked.

"I know this goes against my nature," replied Will, "for aren't us Scots supposed to be dour, suspicious of any enthusiasm? But hey, Julius, the best parts of your book are those extraordinary descriptions of early Israel, its life and worship. Who cares if they are products of your imagination?"

"What do you mean?" Julius asked.

"Oh, where you let yourself go," Will said, "especially with stuff before the priests laid their red right hands on the text. It's the 'old priestless day' (P: 136). Here religious worship 'was a natural thing in Hebrew antiquity; it was the blossom of life, the heights and depths of which it was its business to transfigure and glorify' (P: 77). You love the moments of sacrifice and meal-offering, of spontaneous drinking and making merry, of the pure license of festival, full of sex and food and grog. In short, 'the joyous breathing-time from the load of life which a festival affords...' (P: 115)."

Julius was beginning to enjoy himself again, so he plagiarized himself once more:

"In the early days, worship arose out of the midst of ordinary life, and was in most intimate and manifold connection with it. A sacrifice was a meal, a fact showing how remote was the idea of antithesis between spiritual earnestness and secular joyousness. A meal unites a definite circle of guests, and in this way the sacrifice brought into connection the members of the family, the associates of the corporation, the soldiers of the army, and, generally speaking, the constituents of any permanent or temporary society. It is earthly relationships that receive their consecration thereby, and in correspondence are the natural festal occasions represented by the vicissitudes of life. Year after year the return of vintage, corn-harvest, and sheep-shearing brought together the members of the household to eat and drink in the presence of Jehovah; and besides these there were less regularly recurring events which were celebrated in one circle after another. There was no warlike expedition which was not inaugurated in this fashion, no agreement that was not thus ratified, no important undertaking of any kind that was gone about without a sacrifice. When an honoured guest arrives, there is slaughtered for him a calf, not without an offering of the blood and fat to the Deity. The occasion arising out of daily life is thus inseparable from the holy action, and is what gives it meaning and character; an end corresponding to the situation always underlies it" (P: 76).

"O *man*, that's good." Will's eyes were closed in ecstasy, overcome again with his first passion for this book, this man and his writing.

But just then everything became too much for Julius, the strong tobacco and that inflammable liquid the Australians dared call a "drink." The gorge rose in his throat and it was all he could do to reach for the fire bucket before the rainbow shower spurted forth, with the rich aroma of stomach juices and half-digested food.

"*That's* the spirit," Will said, in a moment of Romantic celebration. "You're living it up." He reached for the book before it fell in the bucket. "Look at what you write: 'That perfect propriety was not always observed might be taken for granted, and is proved by Isa. xxvii.8 even with regard to the temple of Jerusalem; "all tables are full of vomit, there is no room." Hence also Eli's suspicion regarding Hannah was a natural one, and by no means so startling as it appears' (P: 72). Then again, 'To be merry, to eat and drink before Jehovah, is a usual form of speech before Deuteronomy' (P: 71)."

But Will had to help a rather shaky and pale Julius back to his seat when the retching had ceased. "Take it easy, perhaps some water is a good idea." He set off on an expedition to find a water container in the cold, darkened kitchen. His toe soon told him where the bucket was; he reached down and found the metal cup hanging on the side, then filled it and brought it back to Julius.

Julius sipped it gratefully, washing away the taste of vomit from his mouth, although the bucket was another problem. Will picked it up, opened the front door, looked both ways, and tossed it far out into the street.

But he was still full of the ecstasy of the moment and unwilling to let Julius miss his excitement.

"There is one other text that I read time and again," he said, "and I am going to do it now. It is one of the most lyrical passages I have read in biblical studies. Concerning Genesis 1-3 you write:

> "In the first account we stand before the first beginnings of sober reflection about nature, in the second we are on the ground of marvel and myth. Where reflection found its materials we do not think of asking; ordinary contemplation of things could furnish it. But the materials for myth could not be derived from contemplation, at least so far as regards the view of nature which is chiefly before us here; they came from the many-coloured traditions of the old world of Western Asia. *Here we are in the enchanted garden of the ideas of genuine antiquity; the fresh early smell of earth meets us on the breeze.* The Hebrews breathed the air which surrounded them; the stories they told on the Jordan, of the land of Eden and the fall, were told in the same way on the Euphrates and the Tigris, on the Onux and the Arius. The true land of the world, where dwells the Deity, is Eden. It was not removed from the earth after the fall; it is still there, else whence the need of cherubs to guard the access to it?" (P: 304).

" 'Here we are in the enchanted garden of the ideas of genuine antiquity; the fresh early smell of earth meets us on the breeze' – that's simply brilliant, Julius. It's saturated with the Romantics. As is this: 'The mythic background gives it a tremulous brightness: we feel that we are in the golden age when heaven was still on earth; and yet unintelligible enchantment is avoided, and the limit of a sober chiaroscuro is not transgressed' (P: 305)."

Julius was starting to feel slightly better, so much so that an old pleasure began to return to him and he dreamed of hiking in the mountains as he used to do so many years before. And he missed the trees. For sure, Tübingen had trees, but they were cultivated, contained, kept within fences whence they wouldn't be able to gather in the night and take over the city, overwhelming the burghers in an arborial coup. He longed for the trees of the forest, which grow as they will and can.

"What about the trees," he whispered, " 'The wonderful trees in the garden of Eden' (P: 305)."

Will took him up, for if priests populated Julius' dreams, then he dreamt of trees in a Scotland bare of hill and valley. His great love was the tree of life. For one last time he quoted Julius's book at length:

> "The Hebrew people had no doubt something more to tell about the tree of life than now appears. It is said to have been in the midst of the garden, and so it seems to have stood at the point whence the four streams issued, at the

fountain of life, which was so important to the faith of the East, and which
Alexander marched out to discover. Paradise, moreover, was certainly not
planted originally for man, it was the dwelling of the Deity himself... Jehovah
does not descend to it from heaven, but goes out walking in the garden in the
evening as if He were at home" (P: 305).

"God's garden," Julius said, "I want to find God's garden again, to walk
the mountains, smell the earth on the breeze, immerse myself in the forest
never to return. I want to sing kitchen prose, gutter rhymes and diverse
songs from the wood. I want to find a place where it rains eleven months of
the year and the trees drip for the other month."

Will opened one slightly sceptical eye and looked at Julius. One minute
he was chundering in a fire bucket and now he was getting sentimental
about the forest. Looks like I'll have to be the practical one, he thought,
keep my eyes on that fresh earth so he doesn't stand in some wild animal's
dropping.

"And roasted meat," Julius said, "fresh deer we have caught, cut up and
roasted over the fire. In fact, this is the only thing I like about the priests,
that they brought about a change from the old practice of boiling meat –
the Passover lamb was not to be eaten 'raw or boiled with water, but roasted,
its head and its legs and its inner parts' (Exodu. 12:9). Much better than
the older Passover practice of boiling (Deut. 16:7). Let our motto be that of
the servants of Eli's sons in 1 Samuel 2:15: 'Give flesh to roast for the priest;
for he will not take sodden flesh of thee, but raw'."

Saliva shot into Will's mouth. "Every time," he said, "I read the
prescriptions for sacrifice in Leviticus 1–7, especially on the peace, sin and
burnt offering, I dream of vast steaks, huge, red, dripping slabs of cow or
lamb or goat slung over a low cooking fire, its coals glowing orange and
yellow in memory of the fire that had raged not long before. All we get at
home is some old mutton from a sheep that has just keeled over."

"You can have those parts," rejoined Julius, "the shoulder, leg and breast.
But my fantasy is to hack up a dead animal from deep in the forest and cut
out its cheeks, tongue and stomach (Deut. 18:3; P: 153–54). And the brain,
yes, the brain! I'll roast *them* next to your vast steaks. O God, that's *good*!"

" 'Meat juice,' as my father used to say," Will said, " 'you mean blood' we
used to say back in our teens, annoyed at the euphemisms he used. But we
need to do this properly, for blood is the source of life."

"Indeed," Julius said:

"The life of which the blood was regarded as the substance (2 Sam. xxiii. 17)
had for the ancient Semites something mysterious and divine about it; they
felt a certain religious scruple about destroying it. With them flesh was an

uncommon luxury, and they ate it with quite different feelings from those with which they partook of fruits or of milk. Thus the act of killing was not so indifferent or merely preparatory a step as for example was the cleansing and preparing of corn; on the contrary, the puring[?] out of the blood was ventured upon only in such a way as to give it back to the Deity, the source of life" (P: 63).

"That's it!" Will said. "Have you any camping gear? A tent, blankets, wet weather gear? My boots are meant for walking."

"In this chest right here," replied Julius, walking over to a massive timber chest. "It's been a while since I used it." Out of the chest emerged camping gear ready to go, as well as some Prussian army issue backpacks. But the clothes were something else. To Will's astonishment, Julius stripped in front of him and decked himself in "green attire" (P: 297), just like the earth at creation.

And to get in the spirit of things, Julius unrolled two army blankets with the perfume of naphthalene, passed one to Will, grabbed a cushion off the chair and lay down before the fire. By the time Will had done the same, still laden with the dirt of travel, Julius' twitching leg told Will that he had passed into his strange world of priests, trees and sheep's tongues.

Chapter 2

IN THE BEGINNING: HERMANN GUNKEL AND FORM CRITICISM

Hermann ran his fingers slowly through the guitar strings, his ear cocked for the slightest disharmony. "Gott in Himmel! I wish I had a glockenspiel" he cursed, strumming once again. There it was, the third string! He tightened the tuning key a quarter turn and tested it again. Fire glistened off a forehead enlarged by a receding hairline. At the bottom end of this impressive, sheer cliff face one could find valuable purchase on the pebble glasses that marked the boundary with the foothills of nose and mouth, although the latter was concealed by the bushy growth of his handlebar moustache.

That's it! Concentrating on the guitar allowed him to forget the cold, or at least his cold back, for with his friends he sat facing a fire that was only just starting to come into its own. At least the fire stopped his dangling member from shrivelling completely to protect itself from the chill. But just when it had a chance to relax, peeking out from hiding and seeking some welcome warmth, Hermann would place the guitar down and put his naked back to the fire. As Hermann massaged feeling back into his somewhat sagging buttocks, his confused penis would begin its retreat all over again.

Seated once again, Hermann picked up his guitar and sang rather tunelessly:

The gift that keeps on giving has come into my house

Like a wild deer at my doorway

He was suddenly so close

The beams are made of cedar wood

The rafters made of fir

The garden holds a fountain, honeycomb and myrrh

I walked along the Broadways

Looking for my love

I asked among the watchmen, "Have you seen my love?"

Promise not to wake him, sisters

Let him sleep his time

He comforts me with apples

Succours me with wine

Holy night, blessed daylight

You are my true delight

"Oh, that's simply wonderful," Sigmund said with a lump in his throat. A naked Sigmund Mowinckel had joined Hermann on this early spring camping trip in the woods of Northern Germany. He had come down from Uppsala in Sweden and while the others shivered, he was enjoying these warmer climes. Unlike Hermann's rather lithe and, to be frank, somewhat desirable form, Sigmund carried with pride the extra padding required for the long northern winters. In his very walk – although many would have called it more of a waddle – he announced to the world, *I am a fine specimen of a human being*. But now he sat by the fire, resembling more a mountain than a human being, beginning wide at the base and tapering away to the top of his head. He might not agree with all that Hermann had written, but he was certainly enjoying his singing.

But not so Rudolph: "That was crap," he grumbled. "And why in the hell should we take our clothes off when it is still so damn cold, you idiot?" Rudolph Kittel was there, coat wrapped snugly around him, largely because he liked Hermann – at least most of the time. They both shared a deep desire to further the still new critical work on the Bible. But this whole camping adventure was not his cup of tea, or rather – since Rudolph never had liked silly English customs such as drinking tea – not his stein of beer.

"It's the spirit of the age," Hermann answered, stepping away a few paces to hug a tree. "The beauty of nature, the fresh spring air when the world comes alive again, the feel of the wind's cold fingers on one's skin..."

"Oh bull!" Rudolph grumbled. He was too much of a Lutheran to let such romantic enthusiasm whisk him into raptures.

"But Goethe here would agree," Hermann answered, turning to an impossibly aged figure.

The greyed and shrunken man sat there, stonily silent and brassily naked.

"He doesn't do or say much" Sigmund observed.

"Oh, he's just absorbing all of this in his own quiet way," Hermann said.

"Maybe the cold has got to him," Sigmund insisted. "Old people feel it so much more. Maybe we should rug him up…"

"No, no, he's fine," Hermann insisted. Goethe had been one of his great inspirations. "Let him be."

"At least we should give him a drink," Rudolph suggested. "In fact, I feel like I've been working a plough. A hard-earned thirst needs a brimming mug of beer, something to warm my heart in this god-forsaken place."

"God-forsaken? *God-forsaken*?" Hermann cried. "But God is here. Can't you feel him present?"

"He'll feel much more present at the bottom of my beer glass, I can tell you," said Rudolph.

Hermann relented and dove into the darkness to roll out a large barrel. Red-faced he reappeared in the firelight. "Give me a hand will you?" he asked. Sigmund raised his bulk and put it to the barrel. It rolled easily into place beside the fire. Hermann retreated again only to return with a hammer in one hand and a piece of metal in the other. Soon he hammered what turned out to be a sharply pointed tap into the base of the barrel. Some of the beer hissed out as the tap slid in, but soon he had it working and was handing out large glasses of beer to the other three. Goethe quietly let his sit at his feet, obviously preferring to leave his drink for a moment.

But Rudolph took an almighty slug that left him with but half a glass and a thick froth around his mouth. "Ah now, that's better," he said, blowing froth over the others and the fire. "So Hermann," he said, "tell us why we're here."

"Weell…" Hermann drawled, sipping on his beer as he preferred to relish its taste and the feel of the bubbles in his mouth and up his nose. "I have had some new ideas and I wanted to share them with you. No-one reads my books or articles and at times I feel like I'm whistling in the dark, pissing into the wind, sounding a lone gong…" The others nodded sagely, being intimately familiar with these metaphors and others. "So I crave a sympathetic ear or two. Or at least ears that will listen and not dismiss my thoughts."

"But Hermann," Rudolph said, barely halfway through his slab, "you run the grave risk of becoming a loner in biblical studies with theories like yours."

Hermann said, "I know, I know. Barely anyone studies my work or comments on it anyway. I really feel as though I'm up a creek without a paddle."

"Ah, but I do," said Sigmund, his face shining with sweat and beer.

"Yes, but you are as daring as I am," Hermann said. "And do people read your work that much?"

"In Norway, some," Sigmund said. "But in Germany, no."

"It's a fine line between epoch-making research and going out on a limb," Rudolph said.

"And between genius and madness," Sigmund added.

"Yes," Hermann joined in. "My early teacher was both. A wonderful instructor, and yet while he taught he developed the strangest theories full of conspiracies and codes and..."

"But we all know those people," Rudolph said, looking at Hermann. "And they always seem to end up in universities. A great, or even a not so great scholar slips past that fine line and becomes an embarrassment, touting some crazy theory that ruins any credibility they might have had."

"But you don't think Hermann is one of those?" Sigmund asked.

"No no, no, of course not..." Rudolph replied. "I have a strange feeling that his day will come. When so many of us have been forgotten, Hermann's crazy theories will take off and we'll be the ones forgotten. But I still can't understand this!" With a sweep of his arm he took in the fire, tents in the gloom, overhanging branches of the forest and the naked men before him in the cold night air. "What has got into you man? What's wrong with a warm fire in your home and a beer in our lap? Why in hell should we need to do this?"

"Ah, but the setting is crucial," Hermann replied. "Let's call it *Sitz im Leben*, the setting in life. If we were in my cosy parlour, sitting in comfortable chairs and knocking back beer after beer until we slipped into a drunken slumber, then we would have a very different view of the Old Testament."

"Well it was good enough for Julius Wellhausen, so why isn't that good enough for us?" Rudolph asked.

"Well, look at what that setting produced!" Herman said.

"A damn good theory that more biblical scholars should follow, I would say," Rudolph grumbled, "especially with the conservative reaction everywhere around us."

"But a very bookish theory all the same," Hermann said, "one that is tied to written sources, scrolls of vellum on which scribes wrote and then passed onto other scribes. It's like Wellhausen himself, sitting by the fire, with a pile of books around him."

"*Aha!*" cried Sigmund from within his comfortable bulk. "Exactly! That's *it*! All far too much of a Western book-view of the Bible, if you ask me. Wellhausen and his ilk just assume that the biblical authors were writers like themselves, writers of books to be precise."

"No, no," Hermann said. "I happen to think Wellhausen was right" – at that Sigmund furrowed his mighty brow – "but only to a limited extent. There were written sources, of course, but they are only late, coming not much before the final texts that we have. And Wellhausen was too good a Lutheran, despite his own misgivings, to give away the place of reason entirely. It is for him the Word, the written word that counts."

"And what's wrong with that?" Rudolph asked before pouring the remainder of his beer down his gullet.

"Look Rudolph," Hermann said, "I know you've spent endless years editing a critical edition of the Old Testament. Mark my words, Kittel's critical edition will be remembered well after you've gone. But what I like about Wellhausen is that other side – his liking for what is fresh and new. Spontaneous worship in response to the moments of life that he finds in the J-source. The vital traditions in the early life of Israel before the priests got their hands on it and turned it into empty formulae and ritual. But like I said, Julius is too good a Lutheran, even here: for him the return to the earliest *written text* is the most authentic expression of the life of faith."

Sigmund lifted a massive buttock and an explosion boomed out from underneath. The fire flared for a moment with the methane. Later he would come to be known by affectionate biblical students as Bullwinkle, and not without reason. "Well then," he said to Hermann, "what are these new ideas you spoke of a little earlier?"

But Hermann was carefully feeling his singed beard. "Wow, man! That was powerful!" he said to Sigmund. "Better to fart and stink a little (or a lot in your case) than bust your bum and die a cripple."

"That," Rudolph said, "is pure poetry."

Goethe said nothing, although he did look a little more shrivelled and his brow had furrowed significantly.

"But your new idea..." Sigmund urged.

"Ah yes," Hermann began. "Our dear Julius Wellhausen was on the right track, although not in the way we might think. You see, what I like about Julius is that he loved the spontaneous life of faith, the fresh dawn of religious expression that was tied to the rhythms of the land and daily life. Earthy, naive, idyllic – those are the Israelites and their texts that he loves. Those passages in Wellhausen transport me into the seventh heaven."

"But," Hermann went on, "these moments of intuition, of a feel for the text, a deep sense of the life lived beneath the text are all too few. Wellhausen is right that the formulation of ritual and doctrine is late and priestly. For doctrine is but a precipitate of the piety and joy and celebration of faith itself. So why, I ask, did he not go further back, to ask what lies beyond those texts or sources he maps out so well? If we do that we find *oral culture* – legends, songs, stories, hymns, psalms, poems. And they are simply everywhere in the Old Testament, I tell you, *everywhere.*"

Hermann was hopping about the fire by now, swept away by the glory and wonder of it all. His arms were flying, hands waving, singed beard bobbing, dick swinging and jiggling.

Soon Sigmund joined him and they danced together, lithe and lumbering bodies lurching around the campfire. "I couldn't agree more!" Sigmund cried. "An *oral* culture!" Throwing his head back, he let fly a deep primal cry. In a moment Hermann added his howl and their combined bellows bounded their way through the trees and valley and into heaven itself. Had there been life on other planets, then they too would have heard it – the cry of men just a little too much into themselves.

Goethe barely flinched, although that might have been the wind.

"What rubbish!" Rudolph spat at the naked dancing couple – a sight one doesn't want to imprint too deeply into one's imagination, unless of course an ageing and bulky Scandinavian and pale slender German cavorting around a campfire is precisely one's thing.

"My theory's rubbish?" Hermann said, coming to a standstill.

"No," Rudolph replied, "you two are!"

"God, I need a drink," Sigmund said, sweat running down his face and back only to form a flowing torrent in the chasm between his buttocks. He stumped over to the barrel and filled his glass, throwing his head back one more time for a deep draught.

"That's more like it," Rudolph said. "But as for your theory, Hermann, not a bad one in principle: tell us more."

Hermann's chest was heaving as he too reached for his still half-full stein. "The key," he said when his pulse had come within a range that allowed him to speak, "is that all" – puff – "these oral traditions fall into" – puff – "specified *Gattungen*, genres that are quite marked and" – puff – "identifiable. The problem is that so far we haven't been able to identify them all. Scholars have pondered them in isolation – you know, some look at the Psalms, others seek to place *The Song of the Sea* in its narrative, the psalms in Chronicles float away from any of the other psalms. What we need to do is look at all of these, throughout the Old Testament, since we can only find genres when we have a few examples – they need to be gathered in their various baskets, so to speak."

"But don't people just make up stories and songs as they see fit?" Rudolph asked. "Why do they have to fit into particular types? What happened to the inspiration, the instinctual response to a situation, the role of the Muses?"

"Oh, that's all there," Hermann replied, seated again and savouring the lager. "But if you write a love song, for instance, then you will use certain phrases – speak of your lover's eyes, her body, how she has stolen your heart, how you can't do without her, and so on and so forth – that are identifiable as a love song. How else would you know if you weren't familiar with that type of song?"

"Yes, yes," Sigmund said, warming his back by the fire, for the sweat had begun to chill. Steam billowed from his body, giving him the look of a divine visitation, albeit one that had enjoyed a fatted calf or three. "Let me use this example: we know that when we hear, 'Although the weather in Frankfurt is now fine, tomorrow there will be rain and wind,' it will not be followed by 'in Hamburg on the other hand there will be hail, brimstone, and fire from heaven, and the rivers will run with blood.' One is of course a discussion of the weather while the other is apocalyptic. Two different genres that we mix at our peril."

"Quite literally in this case," Rudolph said.

"But there is a second point," Hermann said. "Each of the forms we find takes place in a specific setting. So with the stories of the fathers of Israel, would that not have been told around a campfire – just like this one – by an elder? The children would snuggle up to their mothers and fathers, the teenagers quietly groping each other at the back, and the adults listening closely with rapt faces to a story they had heard before. There may be a few embellishments here and there, a joke or two, moments of danger and fear and rescue, a squeal and a giggle from the teenagers at the back."

"That's all very well in theory," Rudolph said, "but give an example or two."

"Let's take Genesis," Hermann replied. "Wellhausen *et al.* admit there are oral traditions before the sources, but these are not really worth studying, not really the concern of biblical criticism. For this I can't forgive Julius: if the earliest and most spontaneous is the best of the Old Testament, and even the most reliable insight into the life of ancient Israel, then surely oral tradition is where even Julius should go."

"But you still haven't given us an example," Rudolph said.

"Patience, patience, I'm getting there," said Hermann. "If we look at Genesis, what do we see?"

"JEDP, of course," Rudolph said.

"Yes, but behind those?" Hermann insisted.

"Oh, I don't know," Rudolph replied.

"Legends!" Hermann cried.

"Legends?" Rudolph repeated. "As in, what is false?"

"No, no, no!" Hermann cried again. "Legend as a *Gattung*, as a genre."

"Let us," Rudolph said, "for the sake of argument grant your point. But what do you mean by legend?"

Hermann replied: "'A popular, long-transmitted, poetic account dealing with past persons or events' (G: viii)."

"Hmmm," Rudolph said, drawing it from deep in his chest so that it sounded more like a grunt. "Not much to argue with there; but why not myth, or fairytale, or...!"

"But they are different genres!" Hermann said with some emphasis. "Myth concerns the gods, but legends human beings."

"I'm not sure I agree with that entirely," Rudolph replied, "but we'll let it pass. Tell us a little more about this legend..."

"Legend is oral and personal." Hermann warmed to his topic, or at least he got warm by the fire while talking. "Legend deals with private matters dear to the people – you know, the stuff of everyday gossip, peccadillos, personal failings, intimate details. Legend has no need for credible witnesses, and so it often reports extraordinary things – God talks with men on earth, people live incredible ages and so on and so on. Above all, it's not history, which I take as written, public, credible, political and believable."

"Hear, hear," cried Sigmund, who had been rather silent for a while. "But why didn't the early Hebrews write history, as so many seem to think? You know the old line – the Hebrew Bible really is the first instance of history writing in the ancient world, apart perhaps from Herodotus."

Hermann took on a strange pose, staring deep into the fire, watching the flames dance. He seemed to bring up something from deep within himself. He spat *that* into the fire and then quoted from a manuscript:

> "Historiography is not an inborn ability of the human intellect. Instead, it arose in the course of human history at a certain point in development. Uncivilized peoples do not write history. Incapable of objectively interpreting their experiences, they have no interest in reliably transmitting the events of their time to posterity. Their experiences become discolored under their hand; experience and imagination intermingle. They are able to present historical events only in poetic form, in songs and legends" (G: vii).

"Sounds like they weren't quite as smart or sophisticated as us then," Rudolph observed. "Children of the human race, Rousseau's noble savage, blah blah blah."

"Far from it," Hermann replied. "It's beautiful stuff. Legend is poetry, touching much deeper truths than prosaic history. It 'seeks to gladden, elevate, inspire, touch' (G: xi). It's no accident, you know, that 'the legends of Genesis have always delighted sensitive readers'; that 'painters have very often taken the material for their paintings from this book' (G: xxiii)."

"But we're not painters or poets," Rudolph reminded him. "We don't sit around in cafés all day, smoking and drinking ourselves to death on cheap wine, waiting for some muse to inspire us. So how do we investigate these poems you call legends?"

"Yes of course, we're scholars," Hermann said with mock seriousness. "But I think 'that whoever overlooks the artistic form of these legends not only robs himself of a great pleasure, but cannot completely fulfil the scholarly task of understanding Genesis' (G: xxiii)."

"Yes, but how?" Rudolph asked again, now just a little exasperated at Hermann's flights of poetic rapture.

"First," Rudolph replied as directly as he could, "we look at the genre, the form, and then we look at the *Sitz im Leben* – remembering that all the time we have behind the texts an oral tradition. But also remembering that Israel received most of these legends from abroad. 'By nature, these stories wander from people to people, from land to land, and even from religion to religion' (G: xlviii)."

"All right," Rudolph grumbled his concession. "I'll grant you that for now, although I'm not sure all of Genesis is oral legend. So maybe some of the stuff in the Pentateuch began in this way – some, but not all. But what about other parts of the Bible?"

"Aha!" Hermann cried, leaping over the fire, singeing some hair in more sensitive parts and not suspecting at all that he may have been given a leading question. "There is another place where oral tradition is all over the text," he said, ensuring he was still in one piece, "The Psalms!"

"The Psalms?" Rudolph asked. Sigmund was now very attentive.

"Is it not true that try as we might, no one seems to be able to come up with a way of making sense of them, of how they are organized. There seems to be some effort with, you know, the Psalms of David or the Psalms of the Sons of Korah. And then we have the five books of the Psalms. And someone else, unsatisfied with all this, then added the superscriptions – a moment in David's life, a musical direction or two. It's all a great mess!" Hermann himself looked a bit of a mess, hair all over the place, other hair singed, body covered in soot, the fire-brand's glint in his eye. " 'The poetry of Israel is sometimes comparable to a glockenspiel. The individual tones resound powerfully and magnificently, but each reverberates by itself so that only the one who is knowledgeable is able to hear the melody which the tones form according to the intention of the artist' (IP: 1). We need to find some order in this chaos."

"Well, I will grant you that," Rudolph said. "None of us seems to be able to make sense of the Psalms. Of course we sing them in church, but even then we seem to choose them according to content – you know, 'The Lord's my shepherd' or 'Blessed is the Man.'"

"Aha!" Hermann cried for the second time. The others braced themselves for another leap through the fire, but instead he dropped down next to Rudolph, who hadn't moved the whole time, instead wondering what in the world he had got himself into. He didn't need to cry like the wolves and hug trees to know who he was.

"That's it," Hermann went on. "We've been looking at all the wrong places – content, bah, author, bah again. Form is the key, *Gattung.*" He spat the last word out, entirely unaware that spitting out words was for non-German speakers a cliché for German as such. He went on: "What looks like a dog's breakfast is in fact nothing of the sort." He took on a fixed look, as though he were quoting from a text deep within him, which in fact he was: " 'The overall picture demonstrates a rich treasury of forms, but at the same time a great strictness of form. All of the deviations constantly revolve around just a few basic forms that remain constant throughout the literary history of Israel' (IP: 40)."

"The basic organizing principle is actually simple," Rudolph said. "We've just been missing it all this time."

"Exactly," Hermann said, "but if we look at the recent studies of folklore, we'll see that oral cultures pass on their stories and songs with a few very basic forms, and then they just play around with these."

"Here, here," Sigmund cried. They all looked over to see what he was referring to, something obviously close by.

After a few moments Hermann said, "Don't you mean 'hear, hear!'?"

"Ja, ja, that's what I meant," Sigmund grumbled.

"So what *Gattungen* do you think are in the Psalms?" Rudolph asked.

"Well, to begin with we have the hymns. There's plenty of those, sung by the congregation in the temple at festivals, celebrations and so on. And then the victory songs, like the song of Miriam by the Sea, or the Song of Deborah..."

"Hold on, hold on," Rudolph cried. "Aren't we talking about the Psalms?"

"Of course," Hermann replied. "But we can't just stay with the book of Psalms, since we find songs all over the Hebrew Bible, from Genesis to Chronicles, and anyone who wants to study them seriously can't ignore all that evidence."

"I'd never thought of that," Rudolph said.

"Of course not," Hermann said. "Biblical scholars are so defensive of their own turf they rarely even venture out of a small section of the Bible. So the Johannine scholars look askance at the synoptic scholars, Pentateuchal scholars grimace at the findings of those who work on the Book of the Twelve. All a bit silly really, like factory workers on a production line."

"What about the other forms?" Sigmund asked around his beer.

Hermann unrolled himself so that he lay on his back by the fire. Oblivious to insects and grubs and spiders that may have come to warm themselves, or perhaps to observe the antics of this strange species, he put his hands behind his head and felt the breeze rustle his chest hairs. "Royal songs," he began to rattle off, "thanksgiving psalms, laments, complaints, hymns, eschatological psalms…"

"But that just sounds like content to me!" Rudolph cried, seizing on what he felt was a slip on Hermann's part.

"But no," Hermann sat up again while a couple of ants explored his left leg. "That's precisely the point! We can determine which is which by very specific structural features of each type, a structure that is remarkably consistent across all of the examples we can find. Content comes into it, of course, but following in the footsteps of form. Now, as for thanksgiving psalms…"

Goethe coughed at this point, and they all froze. Or at least he seemed to cough, for it was hard to tell what Goethe was up to. He was somewhat wizened and shrunken in his old age. His beard blew in the breeze, and his eyes hid beneath his brows. But it did have the effect of stopping Hermann from launching into a long and detailed description of each form. Even the ancient and somewhat zombie-like Goethe found the very thought a little much, especially since he had endured Hermann's banter on too many other occasions.

Rudolph grasped the opportunity. "So who wrote them?" he asked.

Hermann laughed. "Who cares?"

"No I meant, where do they come from?"

"Obviously the life of worship," Hermann replied, "for is that not where we find psalms of praise and thanksgiving, victory and royal songs?"

"Absolutely!" Sigmund cried. "The cult is it. That's where the Psalms belong."

"But I mean something much more specific than that," Hermann said. "The forms themselves have their place in worship. Some forms come from and are used for the celebration, some to respond to calamity. The forms have very specific settings in life."

"Such as?" Rudolph grumbled.

Herman leant forward, eyes sparkling.

> "Let us briefly vizualise an *Israelite festival* in order to understand the festival hymn. On these days, the people came together from near and far to the holy places, but a festival day is a real day of joy. The harvest has been brought in. The country again has grain and wine... How could the people not rejoice and thank its gracious God? So everyone is gathered at the sanctuary in their best clothes and in the happiest mood. They all show off their prettiest jewelry, and it is the day also in which the priests officiate in their festive garments. There, the drunken eyes in the crowd of those appearing see the greatness of Israel in the ancient time, insofar as the king's sanctuary is concerned, and the splendor of the ruler's house... Then, it continues with exorbitant eating and drinking. Indeed, in ancient times, the danger was all too real that the celebration would end in serious riots" (IP: 41-42).

"Speaking of which," Sigmund said, "I'm thirsty." He stood, took a pace away from the fire and squirted a warm stream of piss into the night. Refilling his glass, he stood by the keg for a moment. "But you know, nearly all the revolutions in Europe took place in spring. The sap rises, people get some sun in their undies, visitors from the southern hemisphere think these northerners are the strangest people on earth, and by May Day they're out to change the world. That's why the October Revolution in Russia was so strange. Fancy having a revolution in autumn! Festivals, parties, revolutions and the Psalms!"

"But that's what I call *Sitz im Leben*!" Hermann exclaimed.

"I couldn't agree more," Sigmund said, waving his stein at Hermann.

"But that's not all," Hermann said, jumping up and pacing around once again. "We can't forget the deep individual piety of the Israelites, their joy, celebration and despair at different moments of life. Surely some of the Psalms arose from this context as well: the life of the individual before God. An individual complaint might be sung when things have gone badly – a child dies, a partner leaves, one is sold into debt slavery. But we don't know what these circumstances were in particular since the Psalms use stock phrases, formulae that we find again and again."

"What absolute *rubbish*!" Sigmund cried. "Individual piety *my arse*! You're too tied to Western bookish learning and the tradition of German piety. We've had enough of that in Scandinavia from you Germans. But, since *we* know that where it smells it's warm, and that it only smells when there are other people around, the luxury of individual piety is a luxury of bourgeois Europeans. There is no psalm outside the cult!"

"But have you never felt," Hermann replied, "that moment of awe and wonder, or perhaps of deep despair, of love and hatred, of abandonment and affirmation?"

"Of course I have," Sigmund replied, "but I don't get carried away by it all and write a poem or a song. You're just applying modern models of art and poetry to the Bible and it doesn't work."

"But don't you sometimes look for the words to describe how you feel? Doesn't a novel, or a poem or a picture or even a walk in the beautiful forest allow you to express how you feel?"

"Now you're taking all of your own pietistic assumptions, throwing them in a bag and hurling them into the past," Sigmund said. "You can't assume that human beings are the same in every time and place! Their societies are different; the people are different. We would hardly be able to communicate with them!"

Hermann was crestfallen. Or at least his chin dropped to his chest, the firelight reflecting fitfully off his slightly bald forehead and pebble glasses. His moustache drooped. "So you won't accept that some of the Psalms might have been written from and for the depth and breadth of personal experience?"

"No, I won't!" Sigmund cried. "It's the cult or nothing." He shook his solid Scandinavian jowls to emphasize the point.

"But that's your problem," Hermann rose again to the fight. "You won't give a centimetre. The same applies to your New Year's Festival. You argue that nearly everything in the Psalms hinges around a New Year Festival..."

"But of course," Sigmund cut him off. "Once we have the Enthronement Festival of Yahweh at the centre of the Israelite religion, everything falls into place. At the dawn of the New Year, when the sun passes its winter solstice, Yahweh is re-enthroned in an almighty festival that celebrates the beginning of the New Year."

"I *agree* with you!" Hermann cried, "but only to a certain point. I've written about it only recently you know:

> "...the festival... is one which celebrates the *entry of Yahweh* into his sanctuary. He has become king, and he now enters Zion in order to be honored by his people as king. The voices of those singers accompanying him resound in order to rejoice about the one who is enthroned... In this service, the old year concludes, with its troubles and disappointments, and the new begins with its wishes and its hopes. In this service, one is grateful for the beneficence of the old time and expects the same for the coming year. In this service, Yahweh again becomes king and thus takes possession of his holy place. And so many additional thoughts attach themselves that finally, for the researcher who is

daring and interested in revitalization, this festival appears as the 'most important operation' of all for Israelite religion. Accordingly, one is not surprised that the Psalms as a whole are related to this celebration" (IP: 70).

Sigmund was a little taken aback: "I can't really fault you on that. Do we disagree on this, or not?"

"Ah, but yes," Hermann came back at him. "For you the Enthronement Festival is 'the powerful magnet toward which a large portion of the psalmic poetry is attracted' (IP: 70). So much so, that even eschatology comes from this festival. In fact, you really place 'a heavy load on a very little piece of thread' (IP: 80)."

"But it is the key that unlocks the Old Testament!" Sigmund protested.

"No" Hermann said, "you see 'Helen in every woman' (IP: 72). Your mistake is that you have simply been too loose with the Psalms. You work with *content* and not *form*: if a Psalm has similar content, you connect with others of the same content and before you know it all of them are connected. Only a careful attention to form will avoid this trap. I'll give you Psalms 100, 48, 132, 81 and 15 for your New Year Festival, but that's it! Weeeell, maybe the Royal Psalms. For they

> "were performed in the presence of the king and his dignitaries in the palace or in the sanctuary. The majestic wonder of the room is evident in its venerable splendor, in the expensive, colorful garments of all of the gathered nobles, including the first person of the state in all his ornate dress, in the glittering weapons of his body guards, and in the whirling clouds of expensive incense. One should keep all of this in mind in order to understand this poetry. Then the singer enters this lordly arena, and he strums loudly on the strings and 'his heart overflows with inspired words' (cf. Psalm 45.2)" (IP: 101-102).

"OK, OK, but show us how it works!" Rudolph said, "how does this attention to *form* really work?"

"Alright," Hermann said, getting down to business. He tried rolling his sleeves up at this point, but since he was naked he found that a rather fruitless gesture. So he settled for leaning forward into the fire and bristling his moustache. "Let's take what I have called the complaint psalms, especially the individual ones. 'The individual complaint songs form the *basic material* of the psalter. They stand out from other genres by their number alone' (IP: 122)."

"Why so many complaints?" Rudolph asked. They resonated with him, these complaint psalms, and yet he was just a little suspicious.

"Let's compare them with the thanksgiving psalms," Hermann said. "'There are noticeably fewer thanksgiving songs than complaint songs. Human beings are far less likely to think of God when things are going well than in times of distress, and poor blessed creatures that we are, we more often believe that we have cause to lament and implore than that we have cause to rejoice and be thankful' (IP: 215)."

Hermann paused, looking directly at Rudolph and Sigmund. He gave them the two-finger salute: "But let's get back to the complaints. *Two* things are *vital*. We must look for the form," he said, jabbing one designated finger into the air, "and then the setting" as he poked the sky with the other.

"As for the form," he went on, "we find first of all an introductory cry for help. Embedded in that is a summons to God."

"What's so unusual about that?" Rudolph grumbled. "Wouldn't you call on God if you were in trouble? Even the most non-religious people cry to God for help when they're scared witless in the face of death."

"Absolutely!" cried Hermann. "But don't you think it's strange how such a natural human response has such a stylized form? Again and again in the complaint psalms we find exactly the same arrangement: it begins with a summons encased in a cry for help."

"OK, so what's next?" Sigmund asked, feeling an unaccountable urge to ask another leading question.

Hermann replied: "We get the complaint itself. And it comes in the form of either a narrative or a portrayal."

"Narrative or portrayal?" Sigmund said, echoing Hermann.

"I might be sick, or beset by enemies, or depressed or injured," Hermann said. "So I could either tell a little story – how it is that my enemies had got the better of me – or I could describe the situation – what my illness is doing to me, how I'm wasting away, how I can't sleep at night and so on."

"And then..." Sigmund said.

"Then there is the petition and wish" Hermann said, "you know: Lord, destroy my enemies, give me sleep, destroy or chase away the demon that's making me sick..."

"No different from a prayer," Rudolph pointed out. "Why not just call them petitionary prayers?"

"Two reasons." Hermann's fingers were back up, the one jabbing the air after the other. "One, they were sung; and two, the next item is quite unexpected: it's the rationale for divine intervention. The believer or priest gives a reason why God should help – the petitioner might remind God of past faithfulness, or perhaps that the honour of God's name is at stake, or point out that he will honour God with a vow should the petition be granted."

"Hmmm...isn't that a bit cheeky?" Sigmund said as he walked over to the barrel, his massive buttocks reinforcing his comment with their own seismic shock waves.

"Not as much as the next point," said Hermann. "It's the protestation of confidence: I am your loyal servant, therefore I know that you will answer my prayer."

"What!" Rudolph cried. "No prayerful waiting on God's gracious word, no deference to a far greater being, no awe and reverence?"

"Ha! No!" Hermann spat out. "Forget *that*! Lutherans invented fear and trembling before God."

"Oh, I thought Søren Kierkegaard did that," said Sigmund.

"He was a Lutheran anyway," Rudolph said.

Hermann went on, ignoring his friends: "The psalms of complaint know none of that: they are confident God will answer their petition as they ask."

"Any more?" Rudolph asked.

"No, that's it," Hermann said in a convenient moment of summary. "There's the summons within an introductory cry for help, a complaint in the form of either narrative or portrayal, a petition and a wish, a rationale for divine intervention, and then a protestation of confidence (IP: 153-79)."

"Alright," Rudolph said, having remarkably not lost any of his sharp concentration despite the beer and the naked men cavorting about before him, nor indeed despite the cold of the night air. "But that covers the form of what you call the complaint psalm, but what about the *Sitz in Leben*?"

"Ah," Hermann said, looking askance at the large Norwegian to his left, "this is where I disagree with Sigmund yet again. Originally the complaint psalm belonged to the cult, but this does not mean 'that the psalms *as we have them* which are from this genre show this connection as a whole, or even to any great degree. As evidence, there are more than a few complaint songs that were composed *a considerable distance from the sanctuary*' (IP: 127). Actually, I think many of them were composed while wracked with illness on the sick bed, or by prisoners, or driven by deep contempt of one's enemies, or in bed before going to sleep, tossing and turning with the worries of the day. And it was individuals who wrote them rather than some professional poet."

Sigmund waved a hand of dismissal: "What rubbish! Of course it was a professional poet, employed by the temple and the song's main use was in the cult."

"Sigmund, Sigmund, you sadden me," Hermann said. "I *do* recognize the place of the cult in the complaints, but what we have is a long way from that. There are some communal complaints, you know, and they 'contain the cry of doubt and the cry for help of a tormented people whose own sacred perceptions have also been offended. It is a complaint so heart-rending and at the same time so lingering that it will perhaps never again be heard in the world. The glowing breath of lamentation and supplication hit us in the face from these poems' (IP: 87-88)."

Tears glowed in the corners of Sigmund's eyes, and it was all he could do to hug Hermann without saying a word. Rudolph rolled his eyes and looked into the dark of the forest, wondering whether he shouldn't move his tent.

"That's enough, you two," Rudolph finally managed.

But Herman was on a roll. "Oh, but the complaint was only one form. There's also the hymn. It 'was the highest point of the most beautiful and most profound days of Israel during which Israel made known the majesty, greatness, and grace of its God with full delight and in deepest humility. As a result, the fundamental moods of this poetry are *enthusiasm, adoration, reverence, praise, and exultation*' (IP: 47)."

Sigmund was crying freely now.

Encouraged, Hermann went on: " 'Such a hymn of Israel produced the most beautiful blooms' (IP: 48)."

Sigmund wailed some more. Rudolph was simply disgusted at this open display of Romanticism. Where is the steely manliness we need in these times?

Hermann was certainly not showing it. He put his right hand to his left breast and continued: " 'The *beginnings of the hymn* lie in *the oldest period we can reach*, as is generally the case with the religious lyric of Israel' (IP: 61). 'The situation of the hymn, the annual festival, and the victory festival, were repeated innumerable times in the subsequent history of Israel. Therefore, Israel sang the hymn throughout its entire history. The transmitted hymns also range over this vast time period' (IP: 62). And then, when we turn to the thanksgiving song, we find that it 'provides the most beautiful hours in the life of the pious... The fact that these words preserve a *poetic form* is explained by the poetic giftedness of the people' (IP: 200-201)."

"Cut it out, cut it *out!*" cried Rudolph, who by now had had more than his fill...of this drivel, and of quotations from Hermann's new book. "All these forms – you've mentioned the hymn, complaint psalm, enthronement and royal psalms – can't just be pure forms. Don't they mix and mingle like some gathering of twenty-year olds?"

"Oh but of course," said Hermann, "Let's take the Royal Psalms: they 'are thus not really a self-contained "genre"... Rather, royal songs are comprised of a whole series of genres...' (IP: 103)."

"Such as...?" Rudolph suggested.

"Well, you know," said Hermann, " 'they link up with songs of the people, private songs appropriated for public worship, complaints and so on. And then the thanksgiving songs get mingled with hymns and even the prophetic psalms' (IP: 208-209)."

"Wow! Prophetic psalms?" Sigmund threw up his hands.

"Oh *yes*!" Herman said. "Prophetic psalms:

> "An unbelievable *frenzy of joy* overwhelms the pious ones with this confirmation of their faith. Only this kind of frenzy could solve the problem of the most terrible inner tension. It's a particular contrast to the bitter distress, fear, and pain in which they still find themselves. With an incomparable *impatience* that is only comprehensible in this situation, they wait for the complete confirmation that Yahweh will act. It's indeed time... The prophetic imagination hurries to his entry with rejoicing. It indulges in the alluring images of prophetic promises. It comforts itself with the burning hunger of promised triumphs that allow one to forget all the illnesses of this time. The more passionately the enthusiastic piety throws itself into this world so majestically close, the deeper the world of suffering and distress surrounding them sinks away. With their ecstatic eye they see the present as a blessed time though its fulfillment is still quite far away" (IP: 271).

"And you know, these aren't far from the eschatological psalms. Hope is not dry and empty: it is, rather 'a joyful delight, an enthusiastic excitement for the singers... One could make no greater mistake than to depict and combine the details of hope as dry and empty' (IP: 254)."

Goethe sat dead still, some would have said dry and empty, offering a quiet reprimand to the conversation, the enthusiasm and passion of Hermann, the alcohol-fuelled tearfulness of Sigmund and the grumpy party-pooperism of Rudolph.

Except that what Rudolph said next threw everyone: "I'm hungry. What did you think we might eat, Hermann?"

Hermann shook his moustache, which then managed to get his whole head going. "Aha!" he said, "Some venison."

"Where in the world did you get that?" Rudolph asked.

"Oh, back there," Hermann replied, waving his hand vaguely into the forest.

"You mean you shot it. When?" Sigmund asked.

"Yes, a little earlier, while you two were out walking," Hermann said.

"I told you I heard a gunshot," Sigmund said to Rudolph.

"No, no," Hermann said, "With this." He pulled a crossbow out from the gloom and waved it before them.

"I'm impressed," Sigmund admired the beautifully wrought weapon.

"You're an idiot," Rudolph waved him away. "But I *am* hungry. Where's the carcass?"

Hermann's naked bum disappeared into the forest and he re-emerged, dragging a young buck. "Here, give me a hand."

Sigmund stayed where he was, as did Goethe. But Rudolph leaped to his feet, or at least he would have done had he been thirty years younger. Instead he creaked and groaned and hobbled over to grab a leg and drag the dead deer into the firelight.

Hermann crouched down, looked into the deer's dead eyes and spoke some quiet words. "My fellow deer, thank you for this meal. Your death is our life." And to the others he said, "At the last moment he looked me in the eye and he gave me permission to shoot him for our meal. You can never eat meat unless you have communed with the animal and his spirit."

"Oh what rubbish!" Rudolph cried.

"Where's the knife," Sigmund said, a tear welling in his eye. He moved slowly for a big man, especially since he knew that most literary big men in cheap novels moved surprisingly quickly.

Hermann pointed to the side of the tent, still puffing from the exertion, and Sigmund thumped slowly to the spot and found the knife in its sheath. With a glint in his eye, he fell upon the carcass – a little too literally. Thankfully the stag was dead, for it would have certainly have been squashed to death under Sigmund's fall. And so would Sigmund had he not let go of the knife at the last minute. It bounced and lodged itself firmly in the chest of Goethe, who slowly keeled over sideways.

"Oh my God!" Hermann cried. "You've killed Goethe!"

"What a load of crap!" Rudolph said. "Goethe died in 1832, 22 March to be precise. I don't know who this was, but it wasn't Goethe."

Hermann ran into a psychic wall and stood, dead still, staring wide-eyed at Rudolph. "Dead? *Dead*! Johann here has been an old family friend for decades. He's been with us since I don't know when."

Rudolph finally stood up and had a closer look. There was no blood. He prodded Goethe for a minute. His skin was somewhat leathery – dry and wrinkled as though he had been cured. His well-known, magisterial beard was still in place, but it was a little patchy and wispy, and Rudolph involuntarily tugged on it only to come away with tuft in his fingers. But it was the way the knife had lodged in his chest that intrigued Rudolph the most. For it had made a solid *thunk* but then entered barely a couple of centimetres. And when he pulled, it refused to come out. It may as well have been wedged in stone. Or...? He knocked sharply on Goethe's chest with two knuckles. Clonk, clonk, clonk went Goethe's chest, as solid as a tree-trunk.

"You've embalmed him!" Rudolph cried. "He's full of resin. And then you glued his hair back on."

Hermann shook his head desperately. "No, no, no. I did no such thing."

"Well, somebody did," Rudolph said.

Hermann paused, head down. After a long while he said, "My grandfather knew him, loved him, was inspired by him. He couldn't bear it when the great man died, so he switched bodies before the funeral and had him embalmed."

"As you do," Rudolph said. "And I'm sure there were plenty of embalmers about, it being such a common practice in nineteenth-century Germany."

"But he is such an inspiration," Hermann cried, and this time it was the other sense of cried that was operative here, for tears were streaming down his face. "I love him so."

"What, this piece of petrified wood with hair stuck on it?" Rudolph said. "This is great! Not only am I sitting on the edge of the forest on a cold spring night in God knows where, but my company consists of two naked men, a dead deer and the embalmed body of one our greatest minds. Reality is indeed stranger than fiction."

"Would Goethe like some venison?" Sigmund asked.

The others were dumbfounded. Sigmund was completely oblivious to what had just gone on, for while the other two were arguing over Goethe he had dug out another knife and had been engrossed in carving up the deer. His arms were covered in blood and there were splatters from chin to crotch. On one side lay a pile of red slabs, on the other various leftovers – head, tail, lower legs and so on.

As Sigmund erected a tripod out of branches on which to hang the meat to cook, Hermann said, "Julius would have loved this."

"Julius?" Rudolph said, having completed his inspection of the mummified Goethe.

"Julius Wellhausen – who else," Hermann replied. "He had a thing about sacrifices, open fires, barbecued meat... Didn't like the priests much, but he loved a decent slab of meat cooked over an open fire."

"Ah yes, I remember," Rudolph said. "Went on a camping trip with him once. Tell me, why do I end up going camping with other biblical scholars? Seems to be a bad habit of mine."

"Because deep down you really love us all…" Hermann offered.

"Bugger off," Rudolph replied with his usual good humour.

As for Sigmund, all of his considerable energies were devoted to the cut-up pieces of dead deer he had dangling over the fire. "Just like the ancient Israelite temple" he beamed. "All we need is some music and song while the sacrifice cooks."

"Ja, ja, I know, *Sitz im Leben*," Rudolph growled.

"Of course," Hermann cried and leapt for his guitar. And so the sweat and blood covering Sigmund's body became priestly garments while he pranced about the fire cooking the meat. Hermann strummed his guitar and wailed a thanksgiving song drawn straight from the Psalter. Even for Rudolph the tree trunks became pillars of the temple and he thought he could hear the massed voices of the choir singing to stringed instruments. Only Goethe was unmoved. And when the ecstasy had passed the meat was cooked.

In a euphoric state they eagerly seized huge slabs of venison from Sigmund's hands as he removed them from the fire. Blackened on the outside the "juices" – one should really say blood – ran freely down their hands, arms and chins. The glint in their eyes was unmistakeable as they gave into more primal lusts.

Chapter 3

IN THE UNDERGROUND: MARTIN NOTH
AND REDACTION CRITICISM

"Now, where is that key?"

Martin was in a hurry. Gershom and Ivan were due any minute now and he was far from ready. In fact, he had been lost in that other world of thought, one that he entered eagerly and left with great reluctance. And now, of course, the other two were on their way over and he hadn't even checked to see whether there was enough schnapps for the evening.

He dug through his pockets for the fourth time and came up empty. The three of them would have loved to meet regularly for their drink, on the same day of the week maybe, but this would be precisely what the authorities wanted – a Jew and a Polish resistance fighter having a friendly chat with the Professor of Hebrew! So they met when they could, at odd times and places. Tonight it was to be in Martin's basement, in Königsberg towards the eastern border. The war had been going badly for the Germans, with the western front all but quiet and the eastern front a distant dream. Gershom and Ivan had taken heart, anticipating the end at last. They had stepped up their activities, agitating, providing a safe haven for those fleeing the regime – the few Jews that were left, prisoners of war who had eluded their captors, the occasional airman shot down during the endless sorties from Allied Forces. Above all they had increasing contact with the formidable Red Army, the pride of the still new Soviet Republic to the east.

As for Martin, he spent the war writing. He read his Hebrew Bible and he wrote – often hungry, often without his beloved cigars, and, worst of all, often without wine or cognac. The best he could do was brew his own schnapps in the basement. He'd fallen into a workable rhythm. When he was feeling down, which was, to be frank, quite often, he would descend into the bowels of the house and begin the ritual of distilling. A couple of hours of careful attention to cleaning the equipment, getting the temperatures right and setting the brew on its path, or perhaps bottling an older one that had done its work – a couple of hours of this and he would feel much better. So then he would crack open the oldest bottle of schnapps and write. This made him feel really good – fantastic in fact – until the next morning when the depression returned. So he would descend to the basement…

A rap on the window by the cellar door brought him back to this world, the one of rations, taxes and a full bladder. He turned in fright and caught his foot on the mat at the cellar door. It slid aside with a dusty cough.

"Aha!" he cried, "*There* you are." He bent down to pick up the key, feeling the tendons in the back of his knees protest. I must walk more, he thought to himself, but that old leather easy chair is just so damn inviting! He was, to be polite, somewhat stocky, a feat in wartime. No threat of replicating the tower of Babel here, since he did not push into the heavens a great distance. There was only the vaguest memory of hair on his head.

"Strange place to hide a key!" he said as he shuffled the mat back to its place. "Who in the world thought of putting it there?" He took care to ensure the dirt found its rightful home underneath.

"Martin!" called a low, urgent voice from the window.

"Damn!" Martin murmured, coming up to the window in two quick strides. He killed the lights – which they didn't appreciate all that much as they would have preferred just being turned off – removed the blackouts and through the opened window tumbled Ivan's bulk and Gershom's sparser frame, along with a whole street's worth of snow.

"What kept you?" Gershom demanded. "With all the time we had on our hands lounging around beneath your window we were about to make some coffee for the next patrol to come by!"

Before Martin had a chance to apologize, Gershom grasped him in a back-snapping hug. "It's good to see you, old friend!" he said with a huge smile. Steam and snow billowed off him. He doffed his winter hat, replete with earmuffs. Unfashionably long hair tumbled around his ears in tight greying curls.

Martin's back felt decidedly worse for the experience. Mein Gott, he thought, I hope I haven't popped a disk! Who'd have thought such a slight man would have such strength. And he'd obviously had his hair cut recently, so it couldn't be *that*. Just as Martin was catching his breath and gingerly testing his back, Ivan drew him into a hug that would have made a black bear jealous.

"Greetings, greetings; yes, yes," said Ivan, hanging on just a little too long. Some would have described it as more of an embrace, others a vigorous caress.

Martin's back popped. Suddenly it felt better. "Ahhhh," he said, closing his eyes and straightening. It felt as though water was trickling down his spine, releasing all the tension.

"..and this," Gershom said, "is Ninel."

Martin opened his eyes and looked in surprise at a strong, young woman who could hardly have been in her twenties.

"Honoured to make your acquaintance, Professor Noth," Ninel said with a strong Russian accent.

"And I yours," said Martin. "You must forgive me, but I did not see you."

"Ah yes," Ninel said, "but what you don't expect you don't see, especially when it is somebody tumbling through your window in the evening! Especially a woman." The skin on either side of her eyes formed those laughter lines people usually refer to as a twinkle – a distinct look of mischief, the telltale signs of a life enjoyed in whatever circumstances. "I have very much been looking forward to meeting you, since I have heard so much about you."

"But where did you come from?" said Martin with the usual German proclivity for directness.

"Ah yes, forgive me," Ninel said, "I was shot down not far from here, just across the border in Poland, but I managed to parachute to safety. Fortunately, Ivan found me before the German soldiers did."

"But a *woman*, in a fighter plane?" Martin asked.

"Have you not heard of our women's squadron, Professor Noth?"

"The German soldiers fear them above everything else," Ivan said, "since they take the attack where no man would go. The Valkyries…"

Ninel laughed and would have shaken her long blond hair as she did so. But, authorial license aside, her hair was cut short for combat.

"Welcome, then," Martin said, "Ivan and Gershom have told you about our evenings. You're sure it won't be boring for you, Ninel…"

"…Jankowska," Ninel said. "On the contrary, although we have had a slight interruption – this silly war – I am enrolled as a student at the Institute of the Peoples of Asia at the USSR Academy of Sciences. We know your work rather well there."

"Well, that *is* a happy coincidence," Martin said.

"Yes indeed," Ninel laughed, "but only of the sort that writers get away with from time to time, like your Deuteronomist."

"Ha, yes," Martin retorted, "but not what we can get away with in our scholarly work. It's such a shame that if we want to write something creative we have to use a pseudonym! Otherwise people dismiss us as dabblers, as no longer serious scholars. But come! Let's go down into the cellar."

As they talked, Ivan and Gershom had re-installed the blackout – an old blanket that hooked over a series of bent nails. The window itself looked like it had forgotten what a good coat of paint felt like, let alone a new pane of glass – all available resources, and many that were not available, had gone into the war effort.

Second down the stairs just behind Martin, Ninel saw that the cellar, small enough as it was, doubled as an air-raid shelter. Makeshift beds for Martin and Kathleen, a few worn blankets, and only basic foods on the shelves – whatever they could scrounge from the surrounding farms, such as potatoes, beets, honey, a few jars of preserved fruits, some rare and much prized flour and even more highly prized coffee. The old bricks had absorbed a century or so of cigar smoke and talk, and they looked eager to hear more of what these strange creatures might say.

It stank. But that's what makes it warm, thought Ninel to herself.

"Excellent! *Excellent!*" Martin shouted, his spirits lifting at the sight of his beloved brewery. "The schnapps is going well." He peered at a glass demijohn in the corner that gurgled contentedly – much in the way you would expect a septic tank to gurgle, should you ever have the good fortune to see one at work close up.

"But we can't drink that!" Ivan bellowed back. Ninel hoped they wouldn't spend the whole evening shouting. Too much like the seminars at the Institute, where the deaf old professors would bawl at each other until too hoarse to continue.

"No, no," Martin said in a normal tone. Ninel breathed a sigh of relief. "I have some bottled over here that has been maturing. Let me see..." In one corner a motley collection of bottles had that promising look of dust, cobwebs and the tracks and droppings of unknown insects all over them. Martin pulled out an earthenware jar, tapped it and proceeded to open the lid. He sniffed the contents and pronounced: "Let's drink."

They retrieved various drinking vessels from coat pockets, an enamel mug, a china cup with no handle and large chip out of its rim there, and a bowl. Martin pulled a small pile of gauze strips down from the shelf and began handing them around. The others seemed to think this was a perfectly normal thing to do, but to Ninel's puzzled look Martin said, "It's a little lumpy, so we resort to the old Philistine practice of using a strainer in our mugs in order to sift out the blobs of unidentifiable solids."

"Ah yes," Ninel said, "we have one or two of those Philistine mugs in the museum that I curate on a part-time basis. Unlike the Israelites, the Philistines were great beer drinkers, and their beer mugs had strainers at the mouthpiece to filter out the worst of the lumps. In fact, the thesis that

I am working on under the guidance of Professor Igor Diakonoff argues that the Philistines were closer to the origins of human society, for the first efforts at collective human living were the result of the need to make beer and bread. Have not archaeologists found bakeries and breweries cheek by jowl with each other?"

"Alas," Martin said, "we don't have that great civilized drink around here any more. But schnapps will have to do!" He threw some wood in the furnace – the Nazis couldn't appropriate every single piece of wood in the forest, no matter how hard they tried – and they settled themselves on a collection of seating implements that one might call chairs in a wild flight of imagination. Indeed, the odd collection of seats matched the bottles of schnapps in the corner and the drinking vessels for their variety.

"Proost!" said Martin, raising his drink.

"Mazeltov!" Gershom said.

"Up yours!" Ivan cried, forgetting his national greeting over the first drink.

"To the revolution!" Ninel said. The others didn't blink as they took their first mouthfuls.

Ninel spat out a lump onto the floor. "The real stuff, Martin. Well done!" Ivan followed suit but the other two seemed to have missed out on the lucky dip this time. They roasted worn boots by the furnace, enjoying the heat seeping through the cracked leather. Only Ninel had newish boots, although she had donned the garb of locals as soon as Ivan had got her to a safe house. With barely enough footwear to go around, she thankfully hung onto her Red Army issue winter boots.

"What news of the war?" Martin asked Ivan.

Ivan smiled: "You can't get out of tonight's discussion that easily," he said, "but it seems to go well now. The Red Army has turned the tide and is now pressing through Poland, drawing most of Hitler's troops and taking the brunt of the war. The British and now the Americans push hard on the western front, so we'll see. But we're weary of the war, Martin. I for one would much rather talk with you about what you have been writing."

"I don't know how you do it," Gershom said, "every day you write, in the midst of war and shortages."

"Hard to explain," Martin replied, resting his schnapps on his lap. "It's not for my career – ha, what career in this crazy world we have now! – not for some position at a prestigious university. No, none of that. I just have to write. I'm not happy unless I write something every day."

"But without books!" Ninel interjected. "It is bad enough in the Soviet Union, but at least we get the occasional book from England or the United States. And our publishing houses continue to print, even in wartime."

"Now that would be something," Martin mused, half to himself. "The last book I had published was more than two years ago. Max Niemeyer managed to publish it at his press in Tübingen before things became difficult. We have hardly any students, since now training for the ministry doesn't exempt you from military service even if you support the Regime – although there's hardly anyone like that now. And publishers? If the Nazis have had to set up factories to extract oil from rubber, then there's hardly paper for books! But you know what I miss more than anything...?"

"A decent cigar?" suggested Gershom.

"A better strainer?" Ivan said.

"Sex?" Gershom said, out of turn.

"Lenin?" Ninel said with a sigh.

"What, with Lenin?" Gershom asked Ninel.

"Ohhh, yes!" Ninel cried. "He was such a *handsome* man."

"All of the above, even Lenin!" Martin replied, feeling that the focus had shifted ever so slightly from his own concerns. "But still, not quite: I miss more than anything in the world the chance to talk with people about my work."

"That's why we're here," Gershom said.

"And I can't tell you how thankful I am," Martin said in a moment of sugary camaraderie.

"Pthaw!" Ninel spat out another glob, this time onto the old cast iron furnace, where it hissed and bubbled.

"Looks like you're the lucky one tonight!" Ivan slapped her on the back and added, "Welcome to Germany!"

When she had recovered and taken another wary sip, Ninel asked Martin: "What do you use then?"

"Just my Hebrew text," Martin replied. "You know, Kittel's new edition, from a few years before the war. I have few old books, but even then I rarely use them until I have finished writing."

"Just the Hebrew?" Ninel was astounded.

"But the great thing is," Martin went on, having forgotten his drink, "after a while I find my head is clear of what others have said and I can look at the text with fresh eyes."

"Surely you don't believe that!" Gershom accused him. "We Jews do that all the time, read the Hebrew alone, but we know – unconsciously – that the rabbis read with us."

"What's this... 'unconscious'?" Ivan was puzzled, sitting back from warming his large hands by the furnace. He removed a battered beret and placed it carefully on his knee.

"Sigmund Freud...haven't you heard of him?" Gershom asked.

"Yes, we have heard of him in Moscow," Ninel offered. "But he is not very popular there – 'decadent bourgeois theory of the individual' is the official line as far I understand it. Needless to say his works are not plentiful in the Soviet Union. But we *should* be more interested in him, since he fled Hitler and died in London."

"Yes, but *who* is he and *what* did he say?" Ivan asked.

"He is," said Gershom, "or rather was, a Jewish doctor who discovered – some would say invented – a whole new dimension of human existence – the unconscious. It makes itself known in those odd moments of *déjà vu*, when we say something we don't mean, in jokes...you know, those unexplainable things that we do and yet we can't explain. But Freud's theory is that this unconscious is more powerful than our conscious lives."

"Didn't he write a book on Moses?" Martin asked.

"Indeed he did," Gershom replied, "the last one before he died. It's a bit wacky – Moses was an Egyptian, or rather, there were two Moseses, or Mosi – I'm not sure – and then the tribe murdered one of them and turned him into a god – but I think the book's day will come."

"Ha!" Martin laughed, "Sounds a bit far-fetched to me – I'll bet he thought most of it up in his dreams... But then, you know, most Old Testament history is little better!"

"Speaking of which..." Gershom said, looking directly at Martin with dark, piercing eyes. "I thought you missed talking with others about biblical studies more than anything else."

"Yes, yes, I know... I'm stalling," Martin laughed, the drink lifting his perpetual sadness.

Feeling light-headed, Gershom said, "We'll have to take it easy with this devil's drink if we're going to make any sense tonight. Now Martin, you've avoided us for long enough and yet you've been as prolific as ever. You know, like Ivan, I've read most of it – the *Geschichte der Israels*, and then your *Überlieferungsgeschichtliche Studien* and most recently *Überlieferungsgeschichte des Pentateuch*. I've got some questions for you about them, but tell us, what underlies them all? What insight have you had that has, well, led to an unending stream of ink from your pen for the last few years?"

"They're really monographs rather than books as such, you know," Martin replied. "What I think is that Deuteronomy through to the end of the book of Kings came from one hand, a creative editor left behind in northern Palestine during the exile to Babylon from 587 to 537 BCE. I like this man – all on his own, in retreat in the north. Then there was the other man, the Chronicler, who did much the same thing with Chronicles and Ezra–Nehemiah later in the Persian era. The Pentateuch, or really the Tetrateuch, the first four books, shows signs of having been gathered in a similar fashion, but perhaps by more than one person."

"But have you had a fundamental insight? What's new about your work?" Gershom pushed him.

"Have I had an insight?" Martin repeated, half to himself. "Maybe not an insight, but a feeling of dissatisfaction with biblical studies. You know that Wellhausen, Graf and the others argued for various written sources, especially in the Pentateuch, but elsewhere as well, and that these sources lie behind the text as we have it now. And then Gunkel went a step further and found oral sources – in legend, myth, folktale, laws, music and song and so on, especially in the Psalms and in Genesis – that he felt went back earlier that the written sources. I agree with them to some extent, that there were written and oral sources in some sense or another. All this is very well, in other words, but it is still only preliminary work."

Martin was getting into his zone, as they say, the passion as palpable as the powerful drink he was imbibing. The others were transfixed, although it was hard to tell whether that was because Martin was leaning forward in his chair, his usually detached and withdrawn demeanour giving way to an extraordinary animation, or whether his bald head bobbing this way and that had a strange fascination, or whether indeed it was the effect of the less than conventional drink in a cellar full of the aroma of human living.

Martin would have been about as easy to stop at this point as the Red Army. "They are all giving us the bits and pieces that lie behind the text, as it were, but I want to know how those pieces came to be the text we have. How were the oral traditions and written sources gathered, sorted and arranged?"

"What's new about that?" Ninel interjected. "It was the work of some amateurish scribes, priests who were, to be polite, not the brightest. They weren't quite up to the task, so they threw together odds and ends with no great plan or sense of how things might fit together."

"Well no, I don't think so," Martin answered her, forgetting that the double negative functions in exactly the same way in German as it does in English. "I think there were some very talented and theologically sophisticated individuals who did the job. They gathered what was available and arranged it into much larger coherent wholes, and they weren't at all afraid to add their own materials – you know, summaries, link passages and so on."

"Theologically sophisticated?" Ninel said.

"Of course!" Martin cried with a firm nod. Had he been younger and lived at a slightly later period, he may have developed a career as a television newsreader, given the way he was nodding and affirming his points. "That's the key to their work: they cast all of the material in their possession under an over-arching theological agenda. We might not like their theologies, but theologies they were all the same. But there is one more thing: anyone for a smoke? I need one to concentrate."

"What?" Ninel said, caught in the change in direction.

"Now *that* would be something!" Ivan exclaimed. "What have you got?"

"Not much, I'm afraid," Martin admitted. "No fine cigars, that's for sure. But I did find some interesting looking plants at the edge of the forest and I have dried those leaves. We could try rolling our own cigars."

" 'Interesting looking plants'?" said Ivan, drawing out the words.

"Well yes," Martin said, "the leaves looked smokeable. Anyone willing to try?"

"Why not?" Ivan agreed. "But man, it's getting warm in here." He drew off his jacket to reveal a crumpled shirt covering a once muscled torso – now it was showing signs of softening and expanding. His waist definitely had a larger circumference than his shoulders – but then most men's did.

Martin opened two sealed boxes. Out of one box he drew some larger leaves, still somewhat greenish, and passed them to Ivan and Gershom. Ninel declined to a raised eyebrow or two. From the other box he grasped a clump of shredded leaves, placed it in the middle of the leaf in his lap, spread it out and proceeded to roll himself a cigar. After putting their drinks on the floor, Ivan and Gershom followed his example, and with some experimentation each of them had a lumpy, ill-shapen cigar in hand.

"How do you hold it together?" Gershom asked.

"You'll have to hold it in the right place," Martin replied, "otherwise it will fall to bits."

Martin opened the furnace and put a long twig in it for a moment. He lit the other two cigars and then his own with the flame.

Ivan screwed up his face after a couple of puffs: "This'll be the death of us!" he cried. "Do you know what plant it is?"

"No idea," Martin said, "but it hasn't killed me yet."

So they sat there, a chipped mug of lumpy schnapps in one hand and a homemade cigar made out of some dubious plant in the other, every now and then spitting out furry lumps and strands of soggy "tobacco." They were thoroughly at peace with the world.

Gershom, who had been listening carefully, stood up and turned his back to the furnace. "Roasted the front enough for a while," he said. "Now, I've read your manuscripts – although it took me a while to decipher your handwriting, I must say. Worse than a doctor's script! But you argue that there are three major sections, or at least these are the ones you've worked on: the Tetrateuch, the first four books from Genesis to Leviticus; and then there's the Deuteronomistic History, from Deuteronomy through to the end of Kings; and finally the collection we find in Ezra, Nehemiah and Chronicles – the Chronicler's History as you call it."

"Yes, that's right," Martin said.

"And who wrote them, or rather gathered them together?" Ninel asked.

Martin puffed on his cigar for a few moments, building up a cloud of smoke behind which he felt more comfortable. Wait a minute, he thought to himself, haven't I done this before?

"Martin?" Gershom said.

"Oh sorry, I just had the strangest of feelings, as though I'd been here before, or at least some people were asking me about my work over a drink and a cigar. There was this very persistent guy with a strange accent and he wouldn't leave me alone." He shook his head: "Must have been a dream or something."

"Ah, Freud would call that *déjà vu*," Gershom said.

"Not *him* again!" Ivan cried.

"Who wrote those long texts, Martin?" Ninel said, repeating her question.

Martin paused: "Well, er, the Deuteronomist, the Chronicler, and some unnamed priest for the Tetrateuch."

"My God, Martin!" Ivan jumped in, "you may be a great scholar, but you certainly don't have much imagination! Why not some other names, like perhaps, Dierdrie the Deuteronomist, Christopher the Chronicler and Tom of the Tetrateuch?"

Ninel laughed, "But they're hardly Hebrew names."

"But I'm no Hebrew scholar – what do you suggest?" Ivan asked.

"Daniel the Deuteronomist," Gershom suggested, "Chaim the Chronicler and Pierre the priest."

"Pierre the priest?" Ninel laughed.

"Well you try something in Hebrew that starts with P or T, and it has to look good on paper!" Gershom challenged him.

"Hmmm…good point," Ninel responded.

Martin was aghast. "It's just as well you people aren't writing or editing my books! What would the scholarly world *think* if I started doing such things?"

"What? Like use your imagination?" Ivan said.

"Absolutely," Martin said with yet another nod.

"But that's *it*!" Gershom cried.

"What's it?" Martin said.

"*Editors*!" Gershom replied. "You said you were happy we weren't your editors, but isn't that precisely what Daniel, Chaim and Pierre…" – they all laughed at Martin's look of despair – "I mean, the priest, Deuteronomist and Chronicler – isn't that what they were? Editors. Very skilled and theologically sophisticated editors, like the ones you would want at any press, but editors all the same."

"Yes indeed," Martin said, "that's what I am arguing, that the work of the editor is crucial, that it completes the work of Wellhausen and Gunkel."

"Oh come on!" Ninel cried. "Editor is so…so English! Why not a good German word, like *Herausgeber*?"

"So Martin has invented *Herausgeber Criticism*?" Ivan asked.

They all sat there, somewhat nonplussed. One sipped his drink, another puffed on his cigar and grew just a little more glassy-eyed, and yet another suddenly reached over to put some more wood in the furnace.

"You know," Gershom said, "It hasn't quite got that ring to it, you know like *Gattungskritik* or *Quellenkritik*. Sounds like a department at a press – *Herausgeberskritik*."

"I've *got* it!" Ninel said. "Why not the other word, *Redactor*? – Redactor Criticism."

"No, no, *no*!" Gershom shouted, "*Redactionskritik*, Redaction Criticism!"

Martin paused. "Maybe, but it's so – I'm not sure – New Testament! I didn't call them *Überlieferungsgeschichtliche* for nothing. It's the search for the history of the transmission of the traditions. I'd prefer *Überlieferungsgeschichtlicheskritik*. How would you translate that?"

"Maybe traditio-historical criticism?" Gershom suggested.

Martin smiled. That way his liking for stringing ever-longer words together would be retained.

"You…don't…think that's just a little bit too much of a mouthful?" Ninel asked.

Gershom spluttered over his drink. "Martin is like that – bites off more than he can chew! I still think Redaction criticism has a better ring to it, but we'll let that strange, strange guild of Hebrew Bible scholars be as obtuse as ever."

"Traditio-historical criticism," Ivan pondered. "That's about as sexy as, well, a boot."

"Uh?" Gershom said, "I happen to think boots are very sexy, especially old, old smelly ones."

"Whatever floats your boat," Ivan muttered.

"All right, all right," Martin relented. "You can call it Redaction Criticism if you like. After all, what I am interested in is the work of the Redactor."

They breathed a collective sigh of relief, laughed, slapped each other on the back, hugged and kissed...well, not quite, although Ninel did try it with Martin but he was not that keen. They had indeed hit on something.

"This moment will be remembered," shouted Gershom into the fray, "as the moment when Redaction Criticism was born!"

"Oh come on," Martin said, "that's making a little much of the situation – maybe they'll remember Traditio-Historical criticism."

"No, I'm serious," Gershom replied. "Really, I think you have at least made the beginnings, if not established a new direction in biblical studies. So, let's see, I want to know more about Daniel, your Deuteronomist. Who is he? I see a careful and skilled writer, living in the north during the exile to Babylon from 587 to 537 BCE – when most of the scribal elite had gone – gathering his fragments, talking to people, thinking and writing on vellum. Someone with a very conscious and deliberate plan?"

"Of course!" Martin said eagerly, "you can see that he planned the whole work. He lay out the bare bones of a chronology – from the Exodus to the building of Solomon's temple to the exile to Babylon – and then he fills in the details, such as the sequence of places visited during the wilderness wanderings, or the story of the kings of Israel and Judah. And if he has to, he is not afraid to adjust things, cut material out, make things up – like any good story teller, really."

"But why would someone take the time and effort to do such a thing?" Ninel asked.

"Ah," Martin said with a knowing look. "Because he had an agenda, a theological perspective. The most important parts of the whole collection are the speeches or editorial sermons where our Deuteronomist puts forward his views – in the first chapters of Deuteronomy, the second chapter of Judges, the seventeenth chapter of 1 Kings, and a couple of others. Once you read these, their central role becomes clear and we can see how this Deuteronomistic theology saturates the whole work."

"Tell us, tell us," Ivan cried in mock suspense, "we can't wait a moment longer."

"He needed to explain why the conquest and exile to Babylon happened. Why, if God had chosen Israel, did he punish them the way he did?"

"And the punch line is?"

"Because they had *sinned*," Martin said. "It would have to be one of the most gloomy theological perspectives you could imagine. From the moment they set foot in Canaan…no, even before that, in the wilderness, the people had continually disobeyed Yahweh. The shadow of the exile looms over the whole text from the beginning. The only thing that held the punishment off, according to the *Deu-te-ro-no-mist*" – and he said the word with a slow emphasis and a stern look at Gershom – "was Yahweh's patience. But eventually they had to be punished for their sins. Basically it is: follow my laws and you will prosper; disobey them and you will be punished."

"It's *that* grim?" Ninel said, half asking a question and half pondering to herself.

"Completely hopeless," Martin agreed. "There's not an uplifting moment, a shard of hope in the whole work."

"Hmmm… It's not so uncommon today, that theological perspective," Ivan observed.

"I admire you!" Gershom said. "Only a depressive would find such a sad thing, and yet you're not afraid to stare the beast in the face."

Gershom stood, groaning slightly as he did so.

"You're getting old, man!" Ivan laughed.

"I know, I know," Gershom said. "Strange how your muscles get stiffer as you get older. Wouldn't it be wonderful if they became more supple and flexible and didn't sag so much as you aged?"

Gershom paced for a while, rubbing feeling back into his buttocks. Martin peered at them for a few moments and then caught himself. What am I doing? He asked himself. I'm not interested in mens' buttocks! That's what that strange man did when he was interviewing me before. No, remember you old fool: that was a dream!

Gershom stopped, for Martin had been muttering: "Who are you talking with apart from yourself?"

"Oh, my dream again," Martin replied. "Sit down Gershom."

"No, that seat – I guess it's a chair – is a bit hard and I'm getting soft in my old age. But let's think for a moment about this author, this Dan the Deuteronomist. So, not only is he left behind after the exile to Babylon, not only does he live in the north, not only does he compile a carefully crafted document with detailed attention to the texts he had before him, but he is also overwhelmingly pessimistic about the war and the exile. The only explanation, theological to be sure, is that it is all a result of God's punishment." Gershom paused and took a few more paces. Then he turned, stopped and looked at the others, hands clasped behind his back, hair settling around his ears: "Remind you of anyone?"

The others stopped whatever they were doing, which was mostly concerned with administering the stimulant of nicotine and the suppressant of alcohol to their systems in the time-honoured human fashion of damaging your body and deriving immense pleasure from it.

"Oh, *come* on!" Gershom challenged them. In reply they stroked an odd nose, scratched an ear, adjusted their underwear if they were lucky enough to have some at this late stage of the war.

"Is this a trick question?" Ninel asked, "since it reminds me of our Daniel, the Deuteronomist."

"No, no, no, who else do you know like this – a writer, a scholar, somewhat isolated during wartime, who nevertheless spends his time writing?"

"You don't mean Martin here?" Ivan asked.

"Of *course* I mean Martin!" Gershom cried, throwing his arms wide.

"So," Ninel said, "you think he has – unconsciously as you would say – modelled his Deuteronomist on himself."

"Well, what do you think?" Gershom asked.

"It's not very scholarly," said Ninel, "to let your subjectivity creep into your scholarship. That's tantamount to saying that Martin's work on the Hebrew Bible is autobiographical, at least to some degree."

Martin was not impressed. "You know I try my damnedest to be as objective as possible, writing in careful scholarly prose that squeezes every last possible trace of myself out of my texts. My God, in Germany we regard even the isolated *ich* a dreadful relaxation of scholarly rigour."

"Well, I disagree Martin," said Gershom. "You can't avoid some trace of yourself in your work, no matter how hard you try. In fact, the harder you try the more you find yourself in your text in all sorts of unexpected ways."

"It all sounds a bit, well, fanciful to me," Ninel said. "You speak as though you come from another world, Gershom. It's weird."

"Too much science fiction," Ivan said, "Jules Verne, H.G. Wells...your imagination is too lively."

"Exactly," Martin addressed Gershom with a stern look. "Biblical studies is a science. It's definitely *not* fiction."

"*That* idea," Gershom responded with a prophetic tone, "will be the undoing of biblical scholarship." Still on his feet he walked over to a somewhat startled Martin and began poking him in the chest with his index finger. "Before *you* know it, all *you* will do is talk with other biblical scholars, who will support each other's biases. And you'll start to forget that there are fascinating things happening outside in the world. Whoever heard of doing anything without imagination? My God, biblical studies will become so dull and boring! Worse than political speeches, worse than...than an academic conference!"

The repeated jabbing of Gershom's finger in Martin's chest seemed to press a button that sent blood from Martin's heart to his head and face. If he had been younger he would have jumped or even leapt to his feet. But all he could manage was a more sedate creaking to his feet. Not quite as impressive, but at least he was face to face with Gershom, staring him down.

"What's wrong with academic conferences?" Martin shouted at Gershom, giving him some of his own finger treatment.

Before he knew it he was jabbing Ivan's sizeable chest, for Ivan had expertly inserted himself between the two men, a good head taller than either the stocky Martin or the wiry Gershom.

"Sit down, why don't you," he said gently to both of them. "Martin," he went on, "I'm hungry. What's there to eat?"

The diversion worked a charm. Martin forgot the little fracas instantly. "Well, there's a little cheese and some bread. I could open a jar of preserved fruit and maybe some honey. No Blutwurst, sadly."

He stood, again, and clumped his way up the stairs. Gershom was cooling down, but he remained quiet and contemplated the iron furnace.

"A jar of preserved fruit is like gold these days," Ivan said to Ninel.

"At least you are lucky enough to live in the country," Ninel said, "where you can still get some of these things."

"All underhand," Ivan said, "not quite the black market, but definitely an underground barter system between the town, farms and forests."

Martin's worn boots thumped down the stairs and back into the cellar. He held a wooden board with a small piece of local cheese and some bread that was clearly taking the war as hard as anyone else. Pieces of straw stuck out of a dark crust. But there was another surprise.

"Fish!" Gershom said. "Martin, you're a marvel."

"It's nothing much, really, just some pickled carp from one of the local ponds, but it will do for now."

He put the board down on an overturned box and peered at the cellar shelves. He found a jar of honey and some fruit and placed them on the board as well.

So they settled down to feast on muddy-tasting carp, dry, strawy bread that they dipped in honey, meagre scrapings of cheese and preserved berries from the forest. The schnapps was the ideal complement.

"You know, Martin," Ivan said, returning to their discussion, "you *do* have a liking for individual authors, or perhaps redactors of the Bible – rather than, say, multiple authors and sources, or even groups of editors. Take Chaim, your Chronicler, for instance: he lives in the Persian province of Yehud, far away from the imperial centre, and he, like Daniel the Deuteronomist, gathers his material and edits it into a whole. But you go a step further and argue that he is responsible for both books of Chronicles *and* of Ezra–Nehemiah."

"Similar indeed," Gershom said, a good deal calmer. "Let's put aside my earlier comment for now – although I by no means retract it. What I'm interested in is how you go against Wellhausen, who found Chronicles at least the end run of the cursed bane of priestly influence. For him it was a pure fabrication, characterized by an obsessive concern with the temple and cultus – in other words, the death of vital religion. But *you* think there is something more reliable here – an identifiable source."

"You must mean," Martin said, "the Judahite genealogy that lies behind the genealogies…"

"Ho!" Gershom exclaimed. Everyone looked at him and thought, *what a nerd! Who in the world says "Ho."*

"Ho!" Gershom cried again, just to rub it in. "Martin the sceptic finds a source!"

"What do you mean, 'Martin the sceptic,' " Martin said. He would have had a querulous look in his eye earlier in the evening. But now, after his fifth schnapps, he was feeling the glow – friendly, warm, magnanimous.

Looking at Martin, Ninel thought: if only we could all stop at this point, then we wouldn't have people spewing in the gutter and saying, "*Damn* that was a good night out." But no, we just have to drink on and on and become morose and belligerent. No wonder there are so many wars! Ninel caught herself just in time – my God, I'm starting to sound like a Puritan, and a Soviet one at that!

Gershom said to Martin: "Well, you certainly don't give much credence to sources with Dan the Deuteronomist. One by one the various scrolls, scraps and hastily jotted sources crumble into fragments in your hands. Sure, you say, there were sources, but we can't know anything about them. Or rather, the only sources we have are those that are named – the Book of the Acts of Solomon, the Books of the Chronicles of the Kings of Israel and the Books of the Chronicles of the Kings of Judah. But as soon as you say this you point out that they have been made up from yet other sources. You say they are 'unofficial histories of the kings adapted from official material' (DH: 100), but the problem is that we are now at three removes from the text: sources named in the text are in fact narratives based on older sources. Little chance that we'll be able to find or reconstruct them!"

"Weeell, yes," Martin said, "I just don't think we should get too carried away with things. You know, a good dose of scepticism never went astray."

"Hear, hear!" cried Ivan in a distinctly English moment, for Poles never said "Hear, Hear!" – that was reserved for repressive Englishmen of a certain era, the era of "jolly good, old fellow," the stiff upper lip and other stiff things, although almost exclusively in company of other English gentlemen with less than stiff upper lips.

Gershom pressed on. "But the funny thing is that while you won't give us anything to hang our hats on, so to speak, or our coats or scarves or whatever else" – the others rolled their eyes at Gershom's ability to load a metaphor until it collapsed under the weight – "we do have Dan the Deuteronomist."

"I see what you're saying," Ninel said. "Martin just shifts the point of certainty from one place to another. No sources to speak of, but we can know something about this ancient scholar from his work."

"Exactly," Gershom replied, satisfied that at last someone was starting to see where he was going with all of this. "But, you know, I think that the idea of a Deuteronomistic History is one of your best, Martin. Mark my words: this idea is going to stand the test of time!"

They all raised their glasses – well, at least the implements that held their lumpy drinks – and muttered, "To Martin!" or "To Dan!" or "To Traditio-Historical Criticism!" or even "To Redaction Criticism!" Martin felt a rare warm glow come over him that was not just alcohol, the gift that makes the hearts of gods and human beings glad – and the depression was a memory for the time being.

"Mark my words," Ninel said, "scholars will dissect your work, pull it to pieces and then rearrange it all."

"Absolutely," Ivan said. "They can go in two directions – push the date earlier or later, or see it as a unified or fragmentary work."

"Let's see," Ninel said. "No doubt some will argue for a pre-exilic dating and maybe a secondary editing during the exile, and then others will just see it as all too early; they'll put it in the Persian era."

Martin sighed. "The work of scholarship as normal, I guess, not daring a bold new theory or two."

"And you know..." Ivan said.

"There's more?" Martin cried.

Ivan smiled, teasing Martin. "I wonder if some will say that the odd pieces you see as pre-Deuteronomic – like the story of the ark or the succession narrative from David to Solomon – are actually post-Deuteronomic."

"Or maybe they will argue," Ninel said, "that there is another work entirely – the prophetic record maybe, or a royal narrative..."

"It will get worse, Martin," said Gershom, peering into his mug. "Let me see. What do the dregs of my drink tell me about the future? Oh no!"

"What?" Martin said, thinking the worst.

"Oh my God," Gershom said, "I see a small group somewhere in the north – Scandinavia maybe, oh yes, Denmark – who will argue that there is little if any pre-exilic material, that most of the Old Testament was written in the Babylonian if not Persian era."

"No!" Martin cried.

"*Yes!*" Gershom cried. "And there's more. They will argue that most of it was made-up, a pious fiction with little, if any, historical value. Ancient Israel is a figment of the scribal imagination!"

"Stop, stop, stop!" Martin cried, putting his hands over his ears. "No more!"

"Alright," Ivan said, "But that's the kind of fate in store for anyone who makes a brilliant breakthrough."

"What about Martin's other work," Ninel said. "Why don't you think it will have the same effect?"

"Well," said Gershom, "they start to slip a bit, in my humble opinion."

"What do you mean?" Martin sat up.

"Hmmm..." Gershom said. "Chaim the Chronicler is very similar – an author gathering his bits and pieces and constructing something very new, but you can't resist the temptation to slide back into source criticism. Sure, you focus on the 'devices' and 'attitudes' (DH: 45) of this author as well — the things that drove his editorial work, the selection, combination and then writing of connecting pieces that gave it all an ideological coherence, but this time you just can't resist suggesting a unified source."

Martin hung his head. "You must be referring to the Judahite source in the genealogies."

"Oh no, not the genealogies!" Ninel said, "Enough to cure the worst insomnia."

"Absolutely," Gershom said. "Martin, you argue that there is a source here from Judah – the descendants of Shelah, Hur and Caleb that we find in chapters two and four of 1 Chronicles – and that this old source gives valuable information about Judah that is lacking elsewhere."

"And," Martin joined in, "that it comes from the early ninth century, some five or six centuries earlier than Chronicles itself, not long after the death of Solomon in fact, *and* that it is a military reserve list for Judah."

Ivan was beginning to nod off – a common effect of the dispassionate details of biblical scholarship – but Ninel was alert.

"But why such a source, Martin?" she asked.

Martin was getting excited, which we will assume was excitement over the discussion and nothing else happening in the cellar. "You see," he said, "it gives us an independent source older than the Deuteronomist. So we have chance to recover the history of Judah, the various elements that came into it, such as the Calebites and Jerahmeelites, and then the Qenites, Qenizzites, and Manahathites, all of whom migrated gradually into the land and blended together to become the tribe of Judah."

"But see what you have done!" Gershom said.

"*What*?" asked Martin.

"You are always after something singular, a unity," Gershom replied. "If it isn't an author-redactor, then it's a source you claim to have found. In your work on the Chronicler you try to have your *Blutwurst* and eat it too: there's a solitary editor *and* you come up with a single underlying source."

"But it's only for the genealogies," Martin complained. 'Won't you let me have just a little source?"

"We could do with a little sauce on some of this bread, you know," Ivan exclaimed. "To say it's dry would be giving it a compliment."

"All we've got is some old dripping from a sheep that probably belonged to Methuselah."

"Better than nothing," Ivan said, "where is it?"

"Upstairs somewhere. I'll get it."

"No…you…won't," Gershom said, nodding his head for emphasis with each word. "Ivan, you can go get it. Martin's not getting out of this so easily."

"All right," Martin sighed. "I know where you're heading. By the time I get to the Pentateuch I argue for both a thematic organization of the material and an underlying source that was common to both J and E."

"So what themes organize the Pentateuch?" Ninel asked.

"They're fairly obvious really – guidance out of Egypt, guidance into the arable land, promise to the patriarchs, guidance in the wilderness, and revelation at Sinai."

"Obvious they are," Ninel said, "So what's new about your idea?"

"The difference, at least as far as I'm concerned, is that these five themes actually form the structure of the whole narrative – the other parts are like so many pieces of plaster that fill in the gaps, flesh out the narrative, as they like to say in some parts."

"Ezekiel's dry bones yet again – another allusion," Ninel cried.

"I think it is Ninel," said Martin, "no one's original anymore. They just borrow from somewhere else and pretend it's theirs."

"But what about this source, Martin?" Gershom asked.

"Yeah, what's it *called*?" Ninel asked with the interest that only specialists in biblical studies can muster.

"G," Martin said.

"G?" Ninel asked.

"For *Grundlage*," Martin replied.

"You mean *Common Basis*."

"Yes indeed."

"We can't resist," Ivan called, coming down the stairs with a greasy tin of solidified old sheep's fat. "We're going to have to call this one Gershom the Grundlage."

Even Martin managed a smile.

"You know," Gershom said, "it's a bit like your argument for sources behind Daniel the Deuteronomist's work: the sources that are obvious are actually not sources but they are based on older sources. So with Gershom the *Grundlage*: J and E aren't really our oldest sources, since they rely on an as yet older source that we then need to reconstruct."

"Isn't that a bit like 'turtles all the way down'?" Ninel asked.

"You mean there's an infinite regression?" Martin asked.

"No," Gershom interrupted. "I don't think that's the problem. In fact, biblical studies is already in this situation – fragments of sources and oral traditions all over the place. *I* think the really interesting thing about Martin's work is the need for a single, unifying feature, whether that's an author-redactor or a source."

Ivan placed the rusty tin full of fat on the furnace, checked to see whether everyone had enough to drink, and stood with his back to the fire. Soon the fat softened, the yellow and brown streaks mingling together within the can, leftovers on the outside melting and dripping onto the iron surface of the furnace.

"Mmmm..." Ivan said, closing his eyes slightly, "nothing like the smell of burning fat!"

"The smell of the temple!" Martin said, with perverse relish, "on a day of sacrifice."

"This is the divine food, you know," Gershom said. "Yahweh would demand the fat – 'All fat is Yahweh's' says Leviticus 3:16 – and it was all his. Forget that silly idea of the divine nectar of the Greeks – *animal fat* is the food of the gods." With that he grabbed the can with an old rag and placed it on the floor between them.

"Ah, now that's better," Martin grunted, dipping a piece of strawy bread in the tin and raising it, dripping with fat, to his mouth.

"Speaking of sauces," Gershom said, "let's get back to this persistent liking you have for singularity and unity."

"But that's just the result of careful scholarship," Martin said. He put his drink down so that he could concentrate single-mindedly on the task of soaking his bread in the sauce of the gods.

"Careful, meticulous, rigorous, painstaking – all of the above, but you still like that singular source and/or author/redactor." Gershom had a liking for occupying both sides of the fence whenever he could. It was fence-sitting taken to a whole new level.

"But surely," Ninel said as some warm yellow fat ran down her chin, "that's where the evidence leads Martin. Why is it such an issue?"

"Let me ask Martin a few questions," Gershom said.

"Not before you've had something to eat, old friend," Ivan said. "As it is the rain has a hard time touching you when you stand upright. You haven't eaten any of this food. Here" – Ivan handed Gershom some bread and dripping – "it's beyond words."

But there was no stopping Gershom's logorrhea now. He simply stuffed a great hunk of bread and fat in his mouth and then talked right around it – or through it. "Martin, so the Deuteronomistic History was written by a single individual in northern Israel during the exile?"

"Yes, well I think we've established that!"

"Would you say the time was somewhat bleak?"

"Of course," said Martin, "the political and intellectual elite were in Babylon."

"So there were few friends and colleagues?" Gershom said.

"Apart from the peasants left behind..." Martin said.

"And the political situation?"

"Rule by a foreign overlord, Persian governors, extra tribute to pay..."

"So Dan the Deuteronomist's bleak theological perspective suits his era."

"It's a damn fine fit," Martin agreed.

"What about the Chronicler – sorry Chaim the Chronicler: again a single author or compiler. Again he is back home, as it were, in Yehud, and he puts together both the alternative history of Chronicles and the accounts of Ezra and Nehemiah."

"Nothing earth shattering here," Martin agreed.

"Would you say his theological perspective is as negative as Dan the Deuteronomist's?"

"It's pretty grim – you know, lots of punishment, skin diseases, bowels dropping out, murdered children and so on – but there's a shard of hope at the end with the call to return to Jerusalem. After all, they are in fact back home."

"It ain't quite so bad, then, even if they are just a province in the Persian Empire?" Gershom said.

"Apparently not," Martin replied.

"Hold on, hold on," Ninel cried. "Aren't we talking about a member or two of a very small fraction – the religious intellectuals – of a very small ruling class which was itself only five percent of the population? So when things look grim, it's actually grim for that class, and when things look a little more rosy, the same applies."

"Spot on, my Marxist friend," Gershom said, "but there's another feature about Martin's work that makes this a very particular exercise – and I don't mean the singularity of his authors or sources."

No one said a word, for they all had their mouths full of stale bread and fat extracted from unknown animals, which made it somewhat difficult to talk.

Gershom held on a moment longer as they chewed away. Then he announced: "*the golden age!*"

They all stopped chomping and looked up, puzzled.

"What the…!" Ninel managed.

"*The* golden age," Gershom repeated.

"You mean when we could eat good cheese, fresh bread and drink cognac?" Ivan asked.

"Or when you could do all night what now takes all night to do," Ninel suggested with a glimmer of a smile on her greasy face.

"No, no, no," Gershom cried, exasperated. "The golden age! The one in Martin's *Geschichte der Israels*, the one he's only just written," Gershom said.

"Yes, yes, I've seen that, or least some copies," Ninel said. "Isn't that the time before the kingship, when there was the tribal confederation – what was it called?"

"Amphictiony, based on the ancient Greek model," Martin said.

"... Yes the amphictiony," Ninel went on, "and then the moveable shrine, the tabernacle, that moved from one tribe to another. But wasn't it also the time when the law was established, during the long process of immigration and settlement in Palestine, and obviously the religion that came to be Yahwism. This was when the first texts were written as well, weren't they?"

"Who said biblical scholars lacked imagination?" Ivan asked.

Martin looked askance at him – this was solid, scientific scholarship.

"Ah, now," Gershom said, ready to spring his final point. "And which nation-state do we know that came from tribal origins, slowly unified into a somewhat cooperative group, but was fiercely independent until very recently? And where do we find a terrible situation today, one that you can only condemn as God's punishment, and one that would make you look back to the tribal past as some golden age? It's Germany of course! I just don't think we can understand Martin's work without that history and present reality as its context. Martin, for better or worse, you can't help but reflect your situation and respond to it! When everything is falling apart, when the Germany you knew has gone to the dogs, then the search for some unifying point becomes so much more important."

"So you really think Martin's work is an expression of his hopes and dreams for Germany itself?" Ninel said.

"In some respects, of course, but that's no criticism, Martin my man," Gershom said. "It's the highest praise." He slapped Martin on the back yet again.

By now the arm-waving and back-slapping that interspersed Gershom's energetic pacing about the cellar were beginning to wear just a little on the others.

"Hey," Ivan cried, "maybe that's not such a bad thing – Germany could well do with a decent dose of hopes and dreams. But let's not get too sentimental here, since you know, patriotism is a fickle emotion and can run in all sorts of directions. And Gershom, sit down, dude – we've got some drinking to do, and not to patriotism, not to Germany or even Poland or the USSR. But to you!"

By now the bread was gone and most of the warm fat, so they set about the remaining food on the plank, dug into the "tobacco" and rolled another cigar or two, and tackled what was left of the schnapps, which happened to be a substantial amount. In fact, it seemed as though the more they drew from the jug, the more it seemed to replenish itself. But this was wartime and anything could happen.

Chapter 4

The Longest Revolution: Phyllis Trible
and Feminist Criticism

Phyllis sipped on a martini, a pink martini, and sighed. My God, these Australians can make good martinis, she thought to herself, and sipped some more. As the drink explored her stomach, she stretched out a lazy leg and perused the slow progress of the Hunter River, settled well down in the river flats at the end of its run. She too settled down, on a balcony at the back of a café in the old river port of Morpeth. Once, well before the river silted up, steamers had come up river from the coal port of Newcastle. Now, in a world short of oil, tons of coal went *down* the valley to be shipped day and night around the world. It was the Hunter's contribution to global warming.

But Morpeth was a treasure, she thought. Still a small town which had one day woken up to the fact that it had a colourful history, that the crumbling sandstone buildings on the single main street were actually quite something, that the single lane wooden bridge crossing the Hunter should stay, and that the theologians on the hill in the grand old residence weren't all weirdos.

She had finished another hard day at the theological college, St. Johns. Thankfully liberal with a good dose of high church Anglicanism, they had brought her out to give a series of lectures. She had come here to claim the Bible back from both the fundos and its secular detractors. Just to the south the fundamentalist juggernaut of the Sydney diocese kept threatening to swamp the Newcastle diocese, which had become a haven for liberals and other thinking believers. Here her message had found a ready audience.

But she knew as well that they had brought her out because of one book that had made her a "name." It was over twenty-five years since *God and the Rhetoric of Sexuality* had appeared, and it had gone off like a bomb. With four simple studies, one on female imagery for God, and the others on Genesis 2–3, the Song of Songs and Ruth, she appeared to reclaim the Bible for women in the church. She did wish at times that some of her other work had been as influential, but she had only recently become reconciled to the fact that few academics have a lasting impact, and those only for one book or one essay. The worst thing to do was to try and repeat that for the rest of one's life.

"Phyllis, Phyllis," a woman's voice called. The accent was German.

Phyllis was beginning to enjoy the company of her thoughts, so she was reluctant to bid them farewell just yet. But she did turn to see a smiling woman make her way around the tables and occasional customers. White hair framed a round face, the hair cut in a modest bob and parted on one side, although it kept falling over one eye.

Phyllis stood to greet her. "Lizzy, it's damn good to see you," she said, hugging Lizzy Fireline closely. Tall and lean, Phyllis towered over the solid Lizzy.

Two others followed, one severely stately and the other relaxed, dressed in baggy pants and a loose tee-shirt. Occasionally she would bump a chair or a customer, entirely unaware that she was doing so.

"Mahalath! Marie!" cried Phyllis, repeating the embrace. "It's so good to see you! How did you get here?"

"Train from Sydney," Mahalath said, "what a ride! Tunnels, mountains, water and those amazing fishing shacks you can get to only by boat."

"Would have to be one of the best train rides in the world," Marie Doilie said, "and I've seen a few."

"But what the...?" Phyllis asked. "In Australia?"

"Oh, I'm thinking of moving here," Lizzy said, her thick German accent solidly in place even after many years in the United States. "What with Bush and the way the USA is going, it reminds me so much of Nazi Germany it's not funny. It's the same story: whip up patriotism, make up some enemy, push through so-called emergency measures, engage in aggressive military expansion, build a police state..."

"Yeah, they've really become paranoid over there, worried about dying in some terrorist attack," Marie said. "More likely to die from eating McDonalds, if you ask me."

"But where will you go?" Phyllis asked.

"Oh, you know," Marie said, "somewhere on the costal mountains south of Sydney maybe. We know someone who lives on Brown Mountain, Val Plumwood is her name, down south near Bermagui. One of the first feminist greenies. Great place, just women, old hippie zone, plenty of time to relax, write and talk."

"But how did you know I was here?" Phyllis asked again.

"We were in Sydney, saw a poster of your work, asked some more and found out you were here."

"Well, I was enjoying a rare moment on my own," Phyllis said.

"Come on, you old grump," Lizzy said, "share a drink with some old friends."

"Friends?" Phyllis looked surprised.

"Well, yeees, I know we've had our differences in the past," Lizzy continued, "but I thought we might put them aside."

"Especially here," Marie said, waving her hand out over the river, the odd boat moored to the shore and the kids jumping off the bridge, even though they weren't supposed to.

"What are you drinking?" Mahalath asked Phyllis.

"Look's like a pink martini," Marie said. "Oh, you old queer!" They all laughed. "But I'm going to have a beer. What about you two?"

"Red wine for me, one of those shirazes," Mahalath said.

"Me too," added Lizzy.

Marie disappeared to the bar and returned with a large glass of dark beer, two glasses, a wine bottle and another pink martini.

"What are you drinking?" Mahalath said to Marie. "It looks serious."

"The barman told me it's a 'schooner of Old,' " Marie replied as she poured the other two a glass of wine and passed the second martini to Phyllis.

"But I haven't finished my first one yet!"

"That's so you don't have to get up for a bit," Marie said, "since I think we'll be here for a while."

"Schooner of Old?" Mahalath asked.

"Apparently," Marie replied, "a schooner is a pint glass, but they call it a schooner since the beer glasses still have a picture of a schooner on them. And 'Old' is 'Old Ale,' thick, dark and, well…I'll see what it's like."

The warmth of the Australian sun had them draping jackets over chairs and reaching for sunglasses. It was February after all and still stinking hot, as the locals would say.

Mahalath lit a cigarette, offered one to the others, and when they refused said, "So tell us, Phyllis, what you've been talking about here and in Melbourne?"

"Oh, you know, saving the Bible from all its 'cultural detractors,' critics and abusers," said Phyllis.

"Sounds a bit like that old fart Schleiermacher," Mahalath said with a stern look, cigarette poised.

"Takes one to know one," Phyllis replied.

"What about feminism?" Lizzy asked.

"What about it?" Phyllis said.

"Well you did write one of the definitive works of what some call 'second wave' feminism," Lizzy pointed out.

"Second wave!" Marie cried and took a long suck on her beer. "Oh, that schooner of Old is good value. But second wave! As if you can put feminism into categories! A convenient way to date what we've been doing. I can hear it now: 'Oh, that's second wave feminism. We're onto third or fourth wave feminism now. All you're doing is useful, laid the groundwork, but those battles are over and we're doing far more interesting stuff now.' "

"The funny thing is," Phyllis said, "it's not generational either. OK, we might say that second wave feminism came out of the sixties and seventies, while third wave feminism was that of the next generation in the nineties. But what about first wave feminism? That sure as hell wasn't something happening in the forties or fifties. It's supposed to go back to the 1890s, you know with Lizzy Cady Stanton, *The Women's Bible*, and all that."

"Hmmm...eighty years from the first to the second wave," Marie said with mock seriousness. "Those women must have had some secret to stave off menopause for so long and give birth to us!"

Mahalath laughed and blew out a cloud of smoke. Lizzy spluttered in her drink and shot a stream of red wine out both nostrils. She coughed, sneezed and snorted, reaching for the napkin. At which everyone laughed even more. Even Phyllis managed a smile.

"Crazy witches!" Mahalath laughed.

"I'm sure more than one of those tweed-jacketed, bearded and bespectacled biblical scholars thought so!" Marie cried.

"Yes, and the men too!" Lizzy added, mopping up the last of the wine she had spilled on her pants.

"It's a bit like the effort to divide us up into groups," Marie said. "You know, divide and conquer: there's reform feminists – the ones who want to recover the Bible in some way as sacred scripture, something where you can have your faith and read the Bible too – and then there's radical separatists – who discard the Bible as hopelessly patriarchal and want to separate from men entirely – and then liberal feminists who want equality between women and men, and then womanists, who criticize feminism as being white, middle class and privileged, and then..."

"And then the conservatives," Lizzy came in, "who feel that patriarchy was necessary at times to ensure the survival of Christianity or Judaism."

"Oh, I thought the conservatives were in favour of various patriarchies because that's the divinely ordered model of creation," Marie said. "It's what God wanted because it's in his word, and that's that. Like I said, divide and conquer. If you can put us neatly into categories, then it's easier to deal with us."

"But I do think we need to hang onto the Bible, reclaim it for ourselves rather than give it up to the radicals and conservatives," Phyllis said at last. "It's just too important to give up like that. Sure gives people like me a headache or two, or maybe a split personality. As I wrote in *God and the Rhetoric of Sexuality*: 'A feminist who loves the Bible produces, in the thinking of many, an oxymoron... After all, if no man can serve two masters, no woman can serve two authorities, a master called scripture and a mistress called feminism.'"

"I agree, you know," Lizzy said. "It's such an ambiguous text. There's a power of liberation in that text – like Thomas Münzer argued and fought against Luther, or Winstanley and the Levellers or the Liberation Theologians. It's not just the text of the reactionaries! It's got so many resources for struggles against racism, sexism, classism, speciesism..."

"Oh, I don't know," Marie said. "It's pretty much saturated with patriarchies of all sorts. If you want to recover spirituality and sensuality for women you've gotta go outside the Bible, pick up all those things repressed, burnt, destroyed and denied by the Church – like Wicca and Womanspirit and Gaia..."

"But don't you think it's got both?" Lizzy said. "I mean, it's one of the most repressive texts we've got, and even more so because it's such an important text. *And* it has provided the language for so many people and movements in overcoming some oppression or other."

"Can you have one without the other?" Marie asked. "If not, I'd rather we dispensed with it entirely and found something else that isn't so problematic."

"A bit hard to do really," Phyllis said. "We can't just forget about it, since so many people won't."

"But Phyllis," Marie asked her, "do you really believe, as you argued two and half decades ago, that a major problem is interpretation, that the commentators and the church have interpreted the Bible in their own interests and that if we go back to the text we can read it in a different way, something that's closer to the text itself?"

"No, that's only half true," Phyllis said.

"Really?" Marie pushed her.

"Interpretation *is* the problem," Phyllis said. "But it's not that the text has some true meaning that awaits discovery, that beneath all those centuries of misinterpretation there is some proper interpretation, some sense of what the text really, actually means."

"What then?" Marie asked.

"Let me put it this way," Phyllis said. "The Bible as a book is mute. It's like a musical score that sits there on the page and does not come to life until the choir-director brings it to life."

"So it's up to the reader then," Marie said. "The reader determines meaning?"

"No, that's too crude," Phyllis said. "Meaning comes from the conversation that takes place at the boundary between text and reader…"

"So, meaning comes from this conversation, as you call it," Marie said, "and you're not after some true meaning of the text, one that has been missed for thousands of years?"

"Absolutely," Phyllis said. "There is no absolute interpretation, no one meaning of a text for ever and ever. Everybody brings to the text certain perspectives, whether they are aware of them or not. They stand in a certain place. They may be male, they may be female, they may be European, they may be African, and they may be Asian. All of that affects the way we read the text. We don't come with a blank mind."

"I'll tell you something," Lizzy said, "the perspective you bring to Genesis is just brilliant, especially the story of Eve in chapters 2–3 from your *God and the Rhetoric of Sexuality*."

"Agreed!" Mahalath cried. "I don't think biblical scholars have really gone back on that: Adam, the one made from *Adamah*, is not a name for a man, the first created being. Rather, Adam stands for an undifferentiated being until the creation of women. Only then do we get woman, *ishah*, and man, *ish*, as differentiated beings."

"And that means," Phyllis said, "that the distinction between the sexes is not primary, that woman is not, at least according to Genesis 2–3, somehow secondary to man."

"But that would make Adam androgynous," Marie said.

"No," Phyllis said, "there's a difference between androgynous and undifferentiated. 'Androgynous' assumes that we begin with the male-female distinction and then combine them in some way – you know, like Plato's myth of the androgynous unity that is split at creation and forever looks for its true partner until it finds it. But undifferentiated – well, that's different! That means the distinction between male and female is not primary. The text seems to tell us that there is some humanity that is more primal, more basic than the differences of gender. And it's a humanity that's intimate with the earth and life…"

"Pooh," Marie said, both in disagreement with Phyllis and at the flies that had begun buzzing around her head. "These bush flies are bad news…"

"Probably all the cattle around here," Lizzy said. "It's a simple equation: cow patties = flies."

"Yeah, yeah," Marie said. "Flies or no flies, in no way should we give up the primary distinction between the sexes! What question do we ask when a baby is born: is it a boy or is it a girl? Not: is it black or white or brown? Not: is it working or middle class? And not even: is it gay or straight or bi? Gender is *it*. Everything flows from there!"

"Rubbish!" Phyllis said. "They're just cultural assumptions. And I think we need to replace them with one in which there is a basic humanity that comes before male or female."

"You're too much of a theologian, Phyllis," Marie shot back at her. "In the end you're going to tell us that that it's God's will or something like that."

"Maybe not quite so bluntly," Phyllis said. "But yes, something like that…"

"But why do you need to save the text?" Marie said. "As far as I'm concerned, the text actually tells a patriarchal truth: men dominate women and they tell stories like this to justify it."

"OK, I openly admit it," Phyllis said. "I am still part of the Church, even if it is with just one toe. And I do think we can read the Bible as a liberative text, especially for women."

"I agree," Lizzy said. "I agree. But how does your feminist reading work?"

"Hold on!" Mahalath said. "I really want to hear this, but I'm busting for a pee" – she said in that quaint American way, although some would have said "too much infurrmayshun" – "and I'm really hungry. So why don't I go and pee and see about some food?"

"Oh yeah," Marie said. "I could eat the arse out of a dead horse!"

"Marie! That's gross!" Lizzy cried.

"It's a good one, isn't it," Marie said. "Heard it on the train on the way up here. Gotta pick up a bit more of the local dialect."

"Oh, but please tell me," Mahalath said. "What do you want to eat? And make it quick, I'm in a hurry."

"Why don't you just go and piss," Marie said to her, "and by the time you get back the food'll be here."

"OK, OK, just ask for a fruit platter," and Mahalath trotted off to the toilet with great relief. She disappeared, somewhat desperately, into the little room with what she hoped was the correct icon. These things varied so much from country to country, she pondered, while enjoying the deep satisfaction that can only come with the sound of piss hitting porcelain at high pressure.

The women had been good to their word, for the table was festooned with plates and cutlery and new drinks for all. A little Last Supperish, thought Mahalath. Marie had risked some local version of the hamburger and was now trying to find it in a pile of what the locals simply called "chips." Lizzy had been tempted by the sound of the steak – a massive slab that left room for nothing else on the 50cm plate. And she had ordered it blue, so that it swam in a red pool that one might euphemistically call "meat juice" – as her father had done when she was a child in Germany. Only Phyllis had restrained herself, going for some rabbit food – a salad that would indeed have kept a vast clan of rabbits fed for a year – and some duck. It was, after all, a pub, and what could you expect in a pub…

"This should keep me going for a while," Mahalath said, pondering her plate. She had been doing much pondering lately, on the toilet, over her plate… This was quite literally a platter with fruit: whole bananas, apples, an orange, a massive slice of watermelon and some weird slimy green stuff. Cut the fruit up? Why bother?

"It's avocado," Phyllis said, noticing her staring at the green stuff.

"Oh," was all she could manage. "And what do you have?"

Phyllis held up the menu and, rolling her eyes, read: "Duck leg from the country!" Unable to contain herself, she burst out laughing.

"You're kidding!" Mahalath cried.

"Does the other leg come from a different village?" Marie said through her laughter. "And the breast, maybe from the city?"

They laughed and ate. Marie found her burger, Mahalath grew to like avocado, Lizzy fortified herself with the half cow and Phyllis found rural ducks rather tasty.

"Where were we?" Lizzy said. "Ah yes, Phyllis was about to tell us how her feminist reading of the Bible works."

"Like I said before," Phyllis replied. "I still believe that the text is often misinterpreted. It might be the result of millennia of misreadings, or one misreading might be established very early on and then influences all subsequent interpretation. And so it's our task to take on the bad readings and offer better ones."

"Like your reading of the Song of Songs in *God and the Rhetoric of Sexuality*," Lizzy said.

"Yes, and like my reading of Genesis 2–3," Phyllis added. "But in the Song of Songs one I argue that the text is a celebration of carnal, sensual love between a man and a woman."

"But that's been argued before the seventies," Marie said. "Goes back to the end of allegorical readings a few hundred years back. Throw out allegory – the Song is about God and the Church, or God and the individual believer, or God and the children of Israel – and you get so-called literal readings."

"But then," Phyllis said, "it was read as a celebration of marriage, or of a couple engaged to be married. It had to be domesticated in some other fashion. I argue that it's about sex and sensuality and there's no agenda of marriage or anything else in it."

"You know that other voices have joined the chorus since you wrote that," Marie said, "and argued that the song is about heterosexual love and may well have been written by a woman. But what I want to know is: why one man and one woman? Is it just women on men? Couldn't it also be women on women and men on men? In all sorts of combinations?"

"True, true," Phyllis said. "Maybe I have tried to domesticate the text. Maybe there is a reading that goes even further, and that may be more persuasive. But that's the nature of rhetorical criticism – persuasion!"

"OK," Lizzy said, "what's this 'rhetorical criticism'? Tell us what you do when you actually read a text. I'm going to insist on this until you actually tell us."

Phyllis sat in silence for moment. "I'm not really interested in questions of date, authorship, sociological context, or practices of related cultures. I study each text as a piece of literature, looking at design and patterns of word use as clues to meaning. It may seem obvious to say this, but Hebrew vocabulary and word order *does* make a difference. Basically, you could say that I like looking at the text very, very closely."

"So how's that different from the New Criticism of the 1950s in the USA and England?" Mahalath asked.

"I'm also interested in how the text and its interpretation are *persuasive*," Phyllis said. "What techniques do they – do we – use to persuade our hearers and readers?"

"OK," Marie said. "So you're reading the text as a persuasive piece of literature and trying to persuade others about your interpretation. Hardly means that's a neutral exercise – you're a feminist aren't you?"

"A feminist and a literary critic all rolled into one," Phyllis said.

"So not really a New Critic after all," Mahalath said, "since the pure New Critics felt that feminism was an unnecessary political agenda imported into the text."

"Oh, I think the New Critics and their close readings come straight out of biblical commentary," Phyllis said. "They pretend that they're neutral, that there are no political or historical or gender issues in their reading.

But that's just a screen for all sorts of gender politics. Biblical critics have been doing that in various ways for centuries."

"But the point is that you really are a feminist literary critic," Lizzy said. "All of what you've said points to that – words, but also plot, character and a good dose of intuition."

"I guess so," Phyllis said. "Even though I was trained as a historical critic – you know, in the grand tradition of Wellhausen, Gunkel and Noth. Not that such questions aren't important, but I've come to find that politics, gender, the history of interpretation and a much greater attention to the test itself are more important."

"Form criticism with a feminist political agenda?" Marie suggested.

"Yes, if you take the literary sensitivities of form criticism and not the concern with *Sitz im Leben*."

"I'll give you all of that," Marie said, "but do you really think we can hold onto the somewhat naïve idea that we can offer a better reading of the text? Doesn't that come awfully close to the idea that we can uncover the true meaning of the text beneath all its misreadings?"

"That's a bit strong," Phyllis said. "But I think there are better readings of texts for theological and political reasons."

"Ah," Marie said, "so a truer reading is one that has, say, feminism, as one of its driving forces?"

"But of course," Phyllis replied. "We're never free from any ideology we bring to the text, so we need to argue that one ideology is indeed better than another. Feminism is far better than patriarchy for instance, since feminism works against sexism, oppression, abuse, and works toward the freedom of women."

"Can't disagree with you there," Marie said. "Problem for me is: a feminist reading shows the text up as irretrievably misogynist and patriarchal. I think there is *something* in the text and it's not particularly good. Nothing can be retrieved from it, and your attempt to rescue it is yet another misreading."

Mahalath lit another cigarette, inhaled with obvious pleasure, and said, "So, it looks like both of you, Marie and Phyllis, agree on feminism, but not on its results. Marie, you want to dump the Bible and Phyllis, you want to hang onto it. But" – she paused a moment since she too had taken public speaking lessons – "what about your later book, Phyllis, *Texts of Terror*?"

"What about it?" Phyllis shot back.

"Well," Mahalath said, taken aback. "You focus on four really awful stories – Hagar, the mother of Ishmael in Genesis 16, Tamar and Amnon in 2 Samuel 13, the daughter of Jephthah in Judges 11, and the unnamed Levite's concubine from Judges 19. Not much to redeem here, as you openly admit: Hagar is cast into the desert, Tamar raped by her half-brother, Jepthah sacrifices his daughter on return from battle because of a stupid vow, and the Levite carves his concubine into twelve pieces after she dies from pack rape."

"But there *is* something we can retrieve from these stories," Phyllis said, leaning forward and vigorously nodding her head.

"You're kidding," Mahalath said. "I thought you were pushing it with your *Rhetoric of Sexuality* book, but now..."

"They're *negative* examples, Mahalath, negative examples." The second martini had fired Phyllis up, so she waved to the waiter for another. Her reserve was gone, gone I tell you. Phyllis was *into* this discussion. Marie whooped, Mahalath puffed and Lizzy, well, she went along for the ride.

"That's why each chapter," Phyllis went on, "begins with a tombstone and an epitaph for the fallen women on this story – Hagar, Tamar, the Levite's concubine and Jephthah's daughter. We need these stories in the canon to show us what to *avoid*."

"Now that's a dangerous argument," Mahalath said. "Why not include every story of rape, violence, bloodshed and mayhem since they can all teach us what to avoid. But isn't the catch that they also become an education in sin? It's a bit like that famous long list of sins – the more sins that appear on the list, the more people think, 'Oooh, is that possible? I didn't know you could do that!' "

Phyllis leapt – although it was really more of a gracious creak – to her feet. What's she up to now, the others thought, eyes wide. She raced off to the bar, since this pub didn't actually have waiters and so her grand gesture to wave for another drink a little earlier had floated uselessly into the heavy summer air of Morpeth.

Back she came, not with a drink but half the bar on a massive tray. Teetering on the edge were various assortments of incredibly healthy bar foods – potato chips, salted nuts, and a bowl of deep-fried balls of something that may have swum in the ocean at some point in the distant past.

It was as though she had never left the argument, talking away while hauling the tray over. "There's much more than that," she said. "I think those canonizers might have been a bit smarter than we give them credit for. They weren't just idiots, apparatchiks of the church doing a half-arsed job."

"What in the hell do you mean?" Mahalath said. "There just isn't enough in the canon for any feminist theology. Like Marie I think we 'must create a new textual base, a new canon... Feminist theology cannot be done from the existing base of the Christian Bible.' "[1]

"Spot on, Rosy!" Marie said. "That's why I wrote *Pure Lust,* since we need to look outside the Bible and the Church to find any positive spirituality."

"There's *more* in that canon than you think," Phyllis said, splashing drinks as she plonked them down from the tray. "We've got to have those texts since they really help the Church come to terms with its own violence."

"Synagogue and Mosque too?" Lizzy asked.

"Of course, *of course!*" Phyllis cried. "In fact, these texts should be in the church's lectionary, read to the people, preached on, thought about and acted upon, rather than buried in some dark corner that only biblical scholars read and write about. They need to be out there, and we need to recognize the uses to which they've been put, and maybe a few liturgies of confession and reconciliation mightn't be a bad idea."

"That's dangerous, Phyllis, dangerous," Marie said. "These stories have a long history of justifying violence against women – you know, throw in the idea that Eve sinned first, that women are the temptresses, corruptors and enslavers of men, like the whore of Babylon in the Apocalypse and we're back with a potent mix that has a two thousand year history."

"I'm afraid I agree with Marie," Mahalath said. "Why do we need to detoxify a text that's been a big, big problem for more than two millennia?"

"Oh yes," Marie said. "And didn't canonization mean that they threw out a load of stuff that was just too problematic – you know like the Acts of Paul and Thecla, or the Gospel of Marie...? Why can't we go outside the canon to find works that are much more positive for women, works that celebrate rituals of body and earth?"

"It's simple," Phyllis said, "if you challenge the texts at the heart of the church and its power, you challenge the church itself."

"Oh, come on Phyllis," Marie said. "They're not just going to roll over and wag their tails."

"I suppose you're right," Phyllis said. "Feminism has been revolutionary in some places, in biblical studies and in some churches. But I'm not sure it always changes people or changes institutions. We're not going to overturn three thousand years of androcentrism in a generation or two. But blow me down if it hasn't made a difference!"

"Wouldn't it just be better to let the church wither away – like Marx's idea of the state – rather than fight battles like these?" Marie asked.

---

1 Rosemary Radford Ruether, *Womanguides: Readings toward a Feminist Theology* (Boston, MA: Beacon Press, 1996 [1985]), p. ix.

"I don't see it," Phyllis said. "When one part fades and dies, another comes to life."

She fished out a dubious ball of deep-fried sea creature, crunched on it thoughtfully and turned to Lizzy. "You've been quiet, Lizzy," she said. "What do you think?"

Lizzy had her feet up, leaning back in her chair and watching the others thoughtfully. "Marie and Mahalath can't find much in the text for feminism," she said, "while Phyllis wants to grab the text before it gets dumped in the recycling bin of history. But you're clever, Phyllis, very clever. You say the text is mute, that it only comes to life when we interpret it."

"Well yes," Phyllis said, "but that's not quite all. I also like to ask: what difference does it make to read the Bible from the point of view of its minor characters rather than its major characters? What happens when you read the Bible in terms of the stories of the losers, rather than the winners?"

"Now *that's* interesting," Lizzy said. "So there is something *in* the text and not just in the eye of the beholder?"

"Ummm…maybe," Phyllis said, "although it needs a beholder to see the different stuff…"

"Well, that's my point," Lizzy said. "It's an old one but needs to be said again and again. The Bible's such a contradictory text: pick a text, a position, an idea, a story, and I'm sure I could find one that contradicts it. The Bible's not mute: it just has so many voices that we can barely hear one over the other."

"Bit like a pub," Mahalath suggested, "where you can't hear a thing because there's so much noise, so many voices all over the place."

"And you even get the music blaring away through and over the voices!" Lizzy added. "You know, those infernal psalms that just keep on repeating themselves over and over and over like some worn-out hit on a jukebox or at a nightclub."

'Yes, yes,' Mahalath cried. 'Oh yes, the Bible's just like a pub, a noisy pub on a Friday night!'

'Bull!' Marie said. 'Don't you think *that's* the problem?'

'What? That the Bible's like a pub?' Lizzy asked her.

'No!' Marie said. 'Don't you think it's a problem that there are, as you say, so many voices in the Bible, all talking over each other? Anyone can use it as they see fit."

"No, no, that's why I love it," Lizzy said.

"Why?" Marie said.

"Because we can always find something that undermines its androcentric perspective, something that gives us liberation rather than oppression," Lizzy said.

"Isn't that what you call challenging *malestream* interpretation?" Phyllis asked.

"Sure is," Lizzy said. She was about to give a long list of her books, beginning with *In Memory of Her*, but then realized it would really be a somewhat cheap advertisement for her works.

Phyllis saved her from her moment of embarrassment with a question. "But do you want to claim the Bible for feminists?" Phyllis asked.

"Of course I do," Lizzy replied. "But the Bible's a tricky book. It's not always folly to the rich; the powerful can find plenty of justification in it."

"That's why it's just too dangerous," Marie said.

"Again, I agree with Marie," Mahalath said.

Lizzy reached over and touched Phyllis' arm. "But *I* agree with Phyllis in the end," she said.

"Now you're contradicting yourself," Marie said. "Surely you don't think the text is mute and needs to be given voice by its interpreters?"

"No, no," Lizzy said, "but I do like Phyllis' hermeneutical principle."

"Her what?" Mahalath asked.

Lizzy turned to Phyllis: "let me put this as simply as possible, Phyllis: what drives you when you interpret the Bible?"

"I've thought about that for a long time," Phyllis said. So she took more time to think about it. At last she said: "Choose life!"

"Oh no!" Marie said, "don't tell me you've joined the anti-abortion lobby with their ridiculous slogan of being 'pro-life.'"

"God forbid!" Phyllis cried, sitting bolt upright.

"But what in the hell do you mean then?" Lizzy asked her.

"We can interpret the Bible's texts for death," Phyllis replied, "for violence, for war, for fear, xenophobia and hatred. But that would just be doing what so many people have done for so many generations. We can pick texts and interpret them in such a way that they become tools for oppression and death. *But* we can also interpret them for *life*! Now the Bible, even those same texts chosen by the dealers in death, become life-giving, full of resources of hope and life."

"An example, Phyllis my dear, an example," Marie insisted.

"The statement in Genesis 1, 'and God saw that it was good,' the celebration of sex in the Song of Songs, the healing stories of Jesus, the myth of his resurrection…"

"OK, OK," Marie said, "point taken."

Lizzy threw herself back in her chair. Her head flew back, her arms wide, the chair tipped and just as Marie lunged to grab her, Lizzy's toe in her no-nonsense shoe caught the edge of the table. *Fantastic!* she said. "Phyllis, at times I've had my doubts about you, about the fact that you are remembered for books that are more than twenty years old, that you love the church too much. But I love this, I *love* this: choose life you say!" And she let rip with a laugh of pure delight. The other patrons looked up, stopped speaking, drinks forgotten. What the...? They thought. "Americans," muttered one. The others shook their heads knowingly: "Americans, yeah..."

"Oh, get a grip on yourself!" Marie said, embarrassed for her sister.

"*Live* a little, Marie!" Lizzy cried.

"What's so good about that?" Marie asked. "Sounds too much like pious claptrap, the stuff that gets spouted forth from liberal pulpits across the country on any Sunday."

"Oh no," Lizzy said, "there's more to it than that." She hauled herself back to four chair legs with her feet. "It's just like my hermeneutics of suspicion. We have to read the text with a profound suspicion for its support of power and oppression, the way it can justify what is racist, sexist, homophobic and so on. But then we also need a hermeneutics of recovery – where we find what is positive in the text, what we can use in our struggles for reform and liberation. But this isn't simple: we need to go through the negative moment first, the hermeneutics of suspicion before we can uncover something positive. It's another way of choosing life!"

"Is it really *your* hermeneutics of suspicion and recovery?" Mahalath asked.

"Well, not really," Lizzy admitted, "but I introduced it to feminist biblical criticism."

"Where's it from, then?" Mahalath asked.

"Oh, I think Paul Ricoeur had the idea and then it turned up in liberation theology," Lizzy said.

"I think you'll find Ernst Bloch – you know, his hermeneutics of hope – was doing it well before Ricoeur," Mahalath said.

"Yes, yes," Lizzy said, getting annoyed with Mahalath. "But I did adapt it and develop it for feminist biblical criticism. And we really are better off with those godfathers."

"Hey!" Phyllis said. "I also bring in a healthy dose of suspicion of accepted readings, especially by male interpreters."

"Yes, it's what I call ideological suspicion of *malestream* interpretations," Lizzy said.

"Absolutely," Phyllis said, "that's where we both agree. And then I look for signs as to how these misreadings might have developed – a word read in one way here, a textual emendation there, the favouring of certain parts of the text over against others. And before long we can start to see that the text really has been adapted, abused and used for another purpose."

"Like, world domination," Marie said. No-one laughed. Not even Marie. "But is it really that easy to separate the wheat from the weeds?" Marie went on. "You make it sound as though we can say, 'well that text or interpretation leads to death, so we'll just put that on one side. We won't forget it; in fact we'll keep it to remind ourselves of our violent past.' And then we can pick the good texts or the good interpretations that give life and hope and say: 'That second pile will be the one that we like. *And* we'll read the first pile in light of the second.' Isn't it just a little too much like the old problem of the canon within the canon?"

"No, no, *no*!" Lizzy cried. "It's even more complex than that. The texts of life – to stay with Phyllis' terms – can't exist without the texts of death. Get rid of the texts of death and we lose the texts of life! So we need to go all the way with the hermeneutics of suspicion, to make that point. But then, only then, can we find our texts of life. And precisely because the texts of death allowed the texts of life to be there, those texts of life can begin to undermine the texts of death, to show that death hasn't got the final say."

"What?" Marie said, somewhat puzzled. "An example, Lizzy my dear, an example."

"The best are the stories of Mary Magdalene in the New Testament," Lizzy said. "What we have now are stories of Mary coming to know Jesus, and yet somehow subservient to him, outside the circle of male disciples. A useful person maybe, but really not trustworthy enough to be part of the inner circle."

"Yes, and then she gets connected with the woman who anoints Jesus' feet with expensive perfume in Luke before he dies and the story of the woman caught in adultery in John 7.53–8.11 – the one where Jesus doodles in the sand and utters those famous words, 'let him who is without sin..',"' said Phyllis.

"The stories of Mary Magdalene wouldn't be there at all if they hadn't been preserved in this form," Lizzy said, "and that's my point. It's not a great picture: she's subservient and useful in a limited capacity, but the stories have survived in some fashion or other."

"Survived?" Marie said. "I'd rather be dead than survive like that!"

"No, no," Lizzy said. "The stories have been twisted, distorted and then made to serve an ideology of a male church. The later version of Mary as the repentant prostitute just carries on the same tendency that began in the New Testament. But if it weren't for those distorted stories we wouldn't know about Mary at all."

"So, let me see," Mahalath said. "You've actually shown us two parts to the hermeneutics of suspicion: what we have about Mary Magdalene is hopelessly distorted, *but* it's only because they are so twisted that we have stories about Mary at all."

"That's it," Lizzy said. "That survival is the positive moment of the hermeneutics that emerges from within the negative: Mary survives because of the bad publicity she gets in the New Testament."

"So what do we do with that then?" Marie asked.

"Now we start asking what's behind the distortions," Lizzy said. "Can we find out anything about the real Mary?"

"You know it's really taking off – this search for Mary," Mahalath added. "Now we have Jane Schaberg arguing for an early Christian movement in which Jesus was just one of a number in a collective, and that the stories we get about Mary show she was a crucial figure in the movement. Forget that crap about them being married – as if Mary could only be recovered by being Jesus' wife!"

They got the heeby jeebies, shivered, and goose bumps ran down spines at the thought.

"But still," Marie said, breaking the moment of horror. "Doesn't it sound a little too much like the search for the historical Mary?"

"True," Lizzy said, "and I think we'll find that Mary is one of a number of women disciples who have been pushed to the outside in the texts we have."

"But aren't you just doing what the historical critics do?" Marie pushed her. "You're looking – you do it in *In Memory of Her* – for a history behind the text that helps explain the history of the text itself. The method's the same; it's just the results that are different."

"Oh my God," Lizzy cried. "You're right! It *is* history, but a new history that doesn't try to use the master's tools?"

"Get serious!" Marie said. "The work you do *is* using the master's tools, the work of the godfathers, but reshaped for your own work. But can we do this? Is it a kind of 'add feminism and stir.'"

"I'm suspicious of that," Phyllis said. "Traditional questions of date, authorship, history of the text and history behind the text – these have been so much part of an androcentric establishment that we really need to leave them aside for a while. That's why I like rhetorical criticism – it gives us a new angle on the text."

"But that's just another method from literary criticism that you've adapted for feminism and biblical studies," Marie said.

"But at least it isn't tainted by a century and a half of male biblical scholarship," Phyllis said.

"No, just half a century of male literary criticism!" Marie said.

"Look," Mahalath said. "I think this is a stupid argument."

The other three stared at her.

"Of course we're going to engage with all sorts of scholarship," Mahalath went on, "and sometimes there are some really good insights in an otherwise terrible method. At other times a really good feminist approach is going to have a bad day and we have to give it a miss. But the *real* problem is not *this*. Rather, it's whether we're going to be apologetic and defend the Bible for the Church and Synagogue – however reformed you might want the Church or Synagogue to be – or whether we're going to hold the Bible *and* the Church or Synagogue to account for its past and present abuse of people in the name of God."

"I couldn't agree more", Marie said. "Biblical scholars, stuck in the stuffy corridors of seminaries of Church, Synagogue and Mosque, have readily let these institutions off the hook, turning a blind eye to exploitation and oppression carried out in the name of the Bible."

"I for one," Mahalath said, "would rather have the Bible as one of the great documents of secular culture rather than as a religious document. It seems to be much easier to do that when you have a Jewish background."

"But we can't just abandon the Church," Phyllis said. "It's just too important to leave to the conservatives!"

"Sounds like a classic case of false consciousness…" Mahalath said.

"If I drink any more of this beer I'm going to be in an *altered* state of consciousness!" Marie announced.

"What's wrong with that?" Mahalath asked her. "Sounds like a damn good idea."

"True," Marie said. She downed – sculled as they say in Eastern Australia – the rest of her beer, which just happened to be most of it.

Marie drew a deep breath, and let out a long, gurgling beer burp. "Oh wow," she said. "I'm done!"

Despite the drinks and the shade and the cool sandstone of the pub, the heat was cranking it way up. They were all sweating freely, pools of moisture gathering on seats and where elbows had leaned on the table for more than a minute, rivulets running down backs and cracks, the delicious aroma of pheromones drifting through the air…

Marie was about to say "damn, it's hot," but realized that may just be stating the obvious.

Down on the old wooden bridge crossing the river some teenage girls and boys had stripped down and were leaping off one of the pylons into a cool, deep river.

The women sat there, silent now with the afternoon effects of alcohol and the Australian sun.

"Oh, does that look good!" Phyllis cried.

"What?" Mahalath said, starting awake from her dozing.

"Come on!" Marie said.

She and Phyllis smiled and got up.

"*Come on!*" Marie cried again.

Mahalath was up too and then finally Lizzy. But by now they had to follow an eager Marie and Phyllis on their way down the slope to the bridge.

Along the single lane bridge with bolted planks and spans, they walked single file on the left, as one does. The occasional car could go no faster than walking pace anyway. The thick planks burned hot on their bare feet. As they drew near to the teenagers, Marie asked one of them, "how's the water?"

"Cold," said a girl with short dark hair, before looking up. She held her breath, eyes wide.

The four women stripped down to their undies, celebrating the pleasure and beauty of mature bodies. The teenagers were just a little grossed out – it was too much like watching their grandparents out for some fun. It was more naked flesh than they had seen for quite a while, and that was saying something.

Marie leapt first, silent until she hit the water. She surfaced, spluttered, pulled her hair out of her eyes and let out a cry of sheer pleasure. She climbed the ladder back onto the bridge, laughing.

"You've gotta be kidding," Lizzy said. "I'm too old for this."

"Of course we are," Marie said, grabbing Lizzy's hand. Phyllis and Mahalath linked up and, holding hands in a chain, they leapt into the water together.

Chapter 5

A Spectre Is Haunting Biblical Studies: Norman Gottwald and the Social Sciences

For the thousandth time, Norm reached for an imaginary pipe between his teeth. Like the phantom limb of an amputee, he longed to suck on it for a moment, to realize it was out, tap it on his heel, peer inside the bowl, pull out a penknife, scrape the bowl and tap it again before filling it with fresh tobacco and lighting it with the flame-thrower of a lighter he used to use.

But he had given up smoking.

After so many years of pleasure, of smoking to his heart's discontent, he had given it up at the tender age of seventy-one. The physical craving had been easy to deal with, and he could even cope with the pitfall of many a would-be ex-smoker – the beer with friends, the hard decision or moment of high stress. But what still got to him were the habits of the pipe. He missed all the little rituals, the minutiae of a smoker's life. Toughest of all, he couldn't even tell the old joke after a gurgling, death-rattle cough: "I've been smoking for fifty-five years and there's nothing wrong with my lungs."

He did, he had to admit, feel far better for not smoking. A little extra weight, the colour back in his face instead of the tell-tale grey pallor, a lungful of clean air.

Norm was sitting with his back against the trunk of one of the giant trees in the park in the Haight – *that* park in Haight Ashbury in San Francisco where the summer of love had happened all those years ago. The houses along the Haight might have been renovated and occupied by the well-heeled since then, the region turned into yet another yuppie zone, but the sun still had some warmth in it on this early day of autumn, the sky an impossible blue you found only on the west coast of the USA – an image that you would want to construct even if it rarely happened.

The sixties, without apology, he thought, drifting off into memories of dropping out, free love, radical politics and Abbie Hoffman's "*The lesson of the sixties is that people who cared enough to do right could change history.*" Well, they weren't quite his memories, but they were someone's memories.

"Norm, wake up!" said Zephyr Lee. "Would you like some camomile tea?"

"What?" Norm snored himself awake. "What was that?"

"Tea, Norm, camomile tea. I've got a thermos here," Zephyr said.

"Oh, yes please!" Haight, dope and free love were gone, but herbal tea remained.

Zephyr passed cups – floral cups – around to the others gathered in the park – Rick Cowley, Davis Philips and Norm himself.

"Mmmmm," Norm said, sipping his tea. "That's good, *really* good."

"This is so good it's not funny," Rick said and smiled. He smiled often, liked smiling often, and his face knew it. Even the thick white hair that sheltered his face smiled as well. "Are you sure there's nothing else in the tea?"

"Noooo, not really," Zephyr replied.

"What do you mean – not really?" Davis asked. Full of *joie de vivre*, Davis found it hard to sit still, pumped with energy for so many things. Porn-star moustache bristling, he would dash off here to find a stick, jump up there to chase a butterfly, and leap somewhere else – since after here and there you run out of directions – for some purpose known only to himself.

"Well, it *does* have an extra zip to it," Zephyr said, "or at least that's what the woman at the shop said."

"*An extra zip*!" Davis cried. "That's a nice way of putting it."

"Let's just say it'll put us at peace with the world, will bring out the love we have for each other," Zephyr said.

"I'll tell you who needs this peace-loving tea," Rick said. "Those war-mongering neo-cons who've decided that the world is theirs to control," Zephyr said.

"Amen," said Norm, sipping his tea.

"It sure moves something deep inside of me," Davis said, feeling the need to take a crap.

"Amen," said Norm again. "Peace," and with that he proceeded to hug them all, passing the peace, albeit without the sloppy kiss that bothered Irenaeus so much those many centuries ago.

"Take it easy, Norm," Davis said. "We're not here *just* to pass the peace – although I'd really like a peace pipe – say how much we love each other and long for a time that's gone."

"Why, what's wrong with that?" Norm asked.

"I don't know about you," Davis said, "but I'm here to dig you about your work. Let me just say – since this tea is really hitting me now – that I'm not sure whether your *Tribes of Yahweh* is a flawed classic or magnificent failure in BS."

"BS?" Norm queried.

"Bull droppings – biblical studies. Can't tell the difference most times!" Davis' eyes lit up.

Norm smiled, completely unruffled. "What do you mean?" he said.

"I'm just not sure," Davis said, "whether there's a real insight in that massive study, or whether it's complete BS."

"Oh, I think Norm was onto something," Zephyr said. "But it's probably not what Norm expected."

"What do you mean?" Norm asked again, peaceful, ready for whatever might be thrown at him.

"Well," Zephyr said. "The first reaction to your book – way back in the late seventies – was that your theory that early Israel arose from a revolution from within Canaanite society was simply misguided. You seemed to be denying all the biblical evidence that Israel came from outside as a distinct social and political body – breaking into Canaan either abruptly or in a much longer pattern of settlement and skirmish."

"That was it," Rick Cowley added. "And apart from this first scandal – that none of the biblical material was actually what it seemed to be – you really rubbed it in by arguing that early Israel was Canaanite through and through."

Davis sipped some more tea and felt very mellow. In fact, he stretched out on the grass for a moment, and the others were struck with wonder, for they had become so used to Davis' antics. "So you were the first to argue that Israel was a Canaanite phenomenon," he said. "Before you all we had was a model of invasion or peaceful infiltration – one put forward by Albright and the Americans and the other by Albrecht Alt and Martin Noth and a bunch of sundry Germans. They thought that these were the complete boundaries of the conversation, firing volleys at each other across the Atlantic. But you just threw the cat among the pigeons and argued that Israel was Canaanite, and that it arose from an abrupt internal revolution in Canaan. After that, all we had to do was complete Aristotle's logical square..." Davis leaned forward and doodled with his finger in a patch of dirt. It reminded him of someone somewhere, idly writing in the sand surrounded by a bunch of men and a frightened woman. But he couldn't for the life of him place the memory. Maybe it was a film, maybe he'd read it somewhere, maybe in an email attachment someone had sent him...

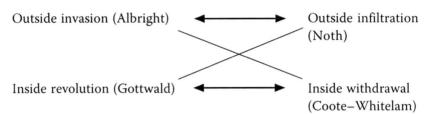

Norm leaned forward and peered. "What's that?" he said.

"Something I picked up," Davis said.

"No, I didn't mean that itchy crotch you can't stop scratching," Norm said. "What are you drawing?"

"Aristotle's table of logical opposites," Davis said, "Greimas' semiotic square, you name it. But it does map out all the possibilities for the emergence of Israel. Two are abrupt and two gradual; two from outside and two from inside."

"And then we can do this," Davis scribbled some more.

"It's a bit like joining the dots," Zephyr observed.

"Loved doing that when I was a kid!" Davis cried, "join the dots to make the picture."

"But Davis," Zephyr said, "why do you think Norm's theory might be flawed?"

"Few people buy the revolutionary hypothesis," Davis said, "or at least the jury is still out on that one."

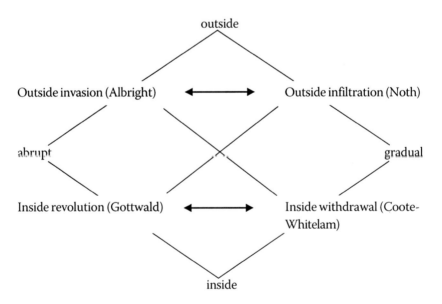

"True," said Rick, "but Norm, you sure as hell blasted out a consensus on the Canaanite origins of Israel. There's not many a Hebrew Bible scholar worth anything who doesn't assume some sort of Canaanite origin for Israel. And there's not too many that take the biblical material at face value these days. Once they took you on for ignoring what the texts said, but now, well, they seem to agree on all of that."

"You're missing the point, guys," Zephyr said. "Canaanite origins – OK, I take that one – and tricky texts – we all agree on that. But it's that whole mode of production thing that is the real secret of Norm's contribution."

"Bloody Marxists," Davis said. "Don't get me wrong – I'm as Marxist as the rest of you – but do we have to have that mode of production narrative? It's so general! Does it mean anything to say that early Israel was a… what was it Norm?"

"A communitarian mode of production over against the dominant tributary mode," Norm said.

"What is *that* supposed to mean?" Davis asked.

"I'd prefer a domestic or household mode of production to communitarian," Zephyr said.

"Yes, but what's it supposed to mean?" Davis said.

"Quite simply," Zephyr went on, "in one, tribute was extracted from the peasants to pay for the state – king's court, priests and their religion, building programs, army, you name it – and in the other one production took place mainly within the family or household."

"OK, I'll buy the tributary, or maybe what others call the Asiatic mode of production…" Davis said.

"Yes, and we can have local and foreign tributary modes – one keeps the tribute within the local state, while in the other one a foreign power extracts tribute from your country on top of the local tribute," Norm said. "The local version operated under the kingship of Israel, and the foreign one when Israel was under imperial control – Babylon and Persia mainly."

"So what's this household mode," Davis said, "and why's it so different?"

"The main point of production takes place in the household," Zephyr said quite simply.

"Household?" Davis questioned.

"The clan, or the gens as they call it in anthropology," Zephyr said. "We'd probably call it the extended family."

"But why is it a mode of production?" Davis asked.

Norm leaned forward, drawing on something deep within. He burped, and then said. "That's better!"

"Mode of production, Norm!" Davis insisted. "Tell me more – it seems such a general term."

"Ah yes, mode of production is 'a combination of the material forces of production (including human physical and mental powers) and the social relations of production, the latter meaning the way that producers…organize their work and appropriate labor product' (HB: 147)."

"Norm, Norm," Davis sighed. "Material forces of production, social relations of production – please explain!"

Patiently Norm explained: "A mode of production is basically the way an economy is organized to produce the necessary and luxury goods for a society to survive. By 'material forces of production' we Marxists mean the basic items of an economy – you know, like minerals, animals, land, fertility, rainfall, the physical things human beings use such as their bodies and minds. Under different modes of production these are organized in different ways. 'Social relations of production' – that means the way human beings work together to produce necessary goods. This is where class comes in, but not exclusively. The same applies here as with material forces: the different ways human beings are organized indicate different modes of production."

"So, let me get this straight," Davis said, "it's the way the basic stuff of life is produced – food, clothing, shelter, birth and raising of children – and the way human beings are organized to do this."

"Yes," Zephyr replied, "and in other social formations, these things are produced quite differently."

"Then when they change you have a different mode of production," Norm said. "Those changes are usually marked by deep rifts and conflicts while the new system comes into place and the old one fights a rear-guard action."

"But how do they change?" Davis asked.

"Usually some internal contradiction breaks apart the old one and a new one that deals with that contradiction takes its place," Norm said. "So with the change from what I call a tributary mode of production to a slave-based one under the Greeks and Romans, the gradual driving of peasants into the ground, often into various forms of subservience to their debt-masters, meant that they could no longer produce sufficient product for the system to survive. So slavery and the slave-based mode of production provided a solution to this: slaves did the work while land-holders did not."

"And the new armies that Greece and Rome had were far more effective too!" Rick added.

"Yes, yes," Norm said, "precisely because a slave-based mode of production enabled new and better armies. That's eventually how Alexander the Great and Pompey conquered the East."

Davis wouldn't let up. "But why do you like the idea of mode of production so much?"

"It gives a really good idea – to my mind the best idea – of historical change," Zephyr said.

"But couldn't the two operate together?" Davis said. "A household mode of production that had to produce enough for itself *and* to pay the tribute?"

"Of course," Norm came in, "and it happens more often than not that one mode of production is dominant and others are subordinate to it. But I wanted to say that what Zephyr and others call the household mode of production is another way of speaking about my communitarian mode of production, since that was based on tribal organization."

"So you think this was Norm's real contribution, Zephyr?" Davis said.

"Absolutely," Zephyr said, "the social sciences in biblical studies have never been the same since. Many of us work with these categories."

"So how does it all fit together?" Davis asked.

"Here's the story," Norm said. "Canaan operated under a tributary mode of production, a local version where the peasants were forced to pay tribute to various local warlords and city-states. A group of people that became Israel threw off the Canaanite and tributary yoke and established a new society based on a very different mode, the communitarian…"

"Like a hippie commune!" Davis said.

"Maybe a bit," Zephyr said. "Actually that's not a bad thought: Israel was the original primitive commune! But we can also call it a household or domestic mode of production."

"Yeah," Norm said, "and then because of external pressures and internal contradictions, the communitarian mode gradually broke down and a local tributary mode was adopted within Israel – the kingship in other words at around 1000 BCE. Many of the texts show the tensions between communitarian and tributary ways of doing things. Judges has stories that probably originally came from a communitarian mode of production – decentralized power, local leaders, tribal organization. But under a tributary mode the king would try to tear loyalty away from the clan and to the king."

"Yes, yes," Zephyr said, "it shows up different notions of family. The state prefers a nuclear family since then its loyalty won't be to the larger clan but to the king – you can see it in Genesis 2–3: 'therefore a man shall leave his father and mother and cleave to his wife.' "

"And all those stories," Norm added, "about the fathers and mothers of Israel in Genesis – you know, Abraham and Sarah and Hagar, Isaac and Rebekah, Jacob and Leah and Rachel and their kids – they're the sorts of things that would be central for any clan or tribal organization."

"And the genealogies!" Davis said, "the genealogies."

"Ohhhh," Zephyr said, "they are so manipulated and constructed it's not funny. Sure, genealogies really count for the clan, but royalty can change all of those to suit their purposes. Break the old genealogical ties and make new ones..."

"But didn't the material we have come from scribes who would have been part of the small ruling class?" Davis asked.

"Of course," Norm said. "The buggers! That's why it's so tricky. They would have had to serve the interests of their masters, but then also had their own agendas as well. To top it off they were probably priests as well."

"Bloody priests!" Davis cried. "But what's the next stage in the story, Norm?"

"After a period as a local tributary mode of production," Norm continued, "Israel gets invaded by one empire after another. In fact they were often at the crossroads or friction points between Egypt and Mesopotamia. So we've got the Assyrians, Babylonians and Persians tramping through one after the other, looting, taking prisoners, removing populations or parts of them – in short ensuring control and tribute, but now to a faraway imperial centre. So Israel falls under a foreign tributary mode and the peasants get hit with a double whammy: tribute to the local rulers and the tribute on top of that to whatever empire was in vogue."

"Then the Greeks and Romans turn up," Rick said.

"This is a new mode of production," Norm said, "what Marxists call a slave-based mode of production. Instead of clan- or family-based production, and instead of tribute, the main way these operated was through a massive slave population that did all the work."

"I disagree," Rick said, "much of the evidence, especially for Galilee where the Jesus movement began and where the Pharisees established themselves, suggests that Hellenization was a thin veneer in the cities – Sepphoris is a good example. In the countryside there was widespread resistance to Greek and Roman rule."

"But didn't they at least impose a slave-based mode of production over the tributary mode?" Norm asked.

"Maybe later," Rick said, "but even the Romans were quite happy to leave the tribute-extracting system in place, even refining it. Now the tribute just went to Rome. Why do you think all those Roman roads were built? It sure wasn't for weekend trips and free trade! What looks like trade was in fact the systematic extraction of tribute. And even the aqueducts were a sign of this, drawing water from the countryside to fill Roman baths where they could wash themselves from rural filth and backwardness."

"What about the massive campaign of 67–70 CE," Norm insisted, "when huge numbers of people were enslaved from Galilee to Judaea? This must have affected things."

"Yeah, you're right there," Rick said. "Maybe it's a case of spasmodic advances in the slave-based mode of production – like in the 67–70 CE campaign – with an underlying tributary system."

"Must have been a mess!" Davis said.

"Sure was," Rick said, "why do you think there were so many revolts? They wanted to oppose the Greek and then Roman domination any way they could – culturally, politically and economically. I'd put it in terms of a profound tension between the newer slave-based mode and a residual tributary mode. In the end the Romans got sick of it all and destroyed Jerusalem in 70 CE."

"Jesuuus!" Davis cried.

"Yeah, and he was one of those rebels too," Rick said, "opposing and challenging the empire."

"I'd add the Pharisees," said Norm. "My theory is that both the Jesus movement and the Pharisees tapped into the communitarian mode of production. It was passed down through the prophets, but they really wanted to create in their own small circles the values and ways of living from the communitarian mode."

"How could they know?" Davis asked. "Talk with the dead?"

"It was there in the texts," Norm said, "that are why they interpreted them the way they did."

"But there is a big difference between Jesus and the rabbis," Rick said. "While the Jesus movement came out of the countryside, from the context of long resistance to imperial dominance, the rabbis were based in the cities. They landed in cities like Sepphoris and Tiberias when Jerusalem was destroyed."

"Let me see," Davis said, "so we have a story: Israel emerged as a household mode of production from a tributary mode. But then it reverted to a tributary mode under the kingship – a local tributary mode – and then to a foreign tributary mode under the imperial control of the Babylonians and Persians. This tributary mode continued under the Greeks and Romans according to Rick, although the slave-based mode spasmodically made headway in the face of huge resistance. And for Norm the Jesus movement was part of that resistance in the name of the old communitarian or household mode of production."

"That's it!" Zephyr said.

Davis paused, "I've just got one huge spanner to throw into all of this. But before I do, I'm so hungry I could… Any ideas?"

"Hey, let's share what we've got," Rick said. "Throw it in the middle and be communal about it. A communal meal: from each according to their ability, to each according to their need…"

"Hey, you old hippie," Davis said. "Too much like the fictional image of the early church in Acts, but why not? What have we got?" And with that he dug in his backpack and came out with a greasy bag. He threw it into the middle.

"What in the hell is that?" Rick cried.

"Fish and chips," Davis said, feeling the saliva run in his mouth.

"Dirty deep-fried shark and genetically modified and pesticide-ridden potato, you mean," Zephyr said.

"Mmmm, sounds *good* to me," Davis said.

"You need to eat better," Norm said. "Here, try some of this." He carefully placed an organic salad and some small peaches on the ground between them.

"Rabbit food!" Davis said.

"And what about some organic Cranapple juice," Zephyr said. "As well as some tofu and asparagus."

"Oh my God!" Davis cried.

"I thought you didn't believe in God," Rick said.

"Shows how desperate I am," Davis said.

"And…" Rick said. Davis held his breath, hoping for some culinary relief. But it was not forthcoming. "Here's some organic ryebread, buttermilk, fresh tomatoes and peanut butter."

"Where the hell did you get this stuff from?" Davis asked.

"Oh, they make it at a commune near me," Rick said. "You know what Massachusetts is like."

"Yeah, I've heard," Davis said.

"And mine came from a Hare Krishna farm near my place," Zephyr said, "from…"

"Let me guess," Davis broke in, "from Massachusetts."

Norm pulled out some enamel plates and cups and passed them around.

"Well then," Davis said, surveying the gathering of food that would even have put Govinda's vegetarian restaurant to shame. "I'll try anything once."

He poured himself some Cranapple juice, filled his plate with tofu and asparagus and spooned out some salad that still looked alive – frighteningly so, especially since he had grown up with the tried and true English approach to vegetables: cook them so they melt on your tongue, as his father used to say, or, as he preferred, so they couldn't jump you and take you by surprise.

"So then," Rick said after swallowing down a piece of ryebread and peanut butter.

"You like a bit of ryebread with your peanut butter, Rick?" Davis asked.

Rick ignored him. "Tell us, Davis," he said. "What's the spanner?"

"What if early Israel simply didn't exist in any sense that we know?" Davis blurted out, crunching his way through the salad.

"What?" Zephyr asked.

"Israel was a construction of later scribes in the Persian period," Davis said.

Rick smiled. "Yes, I remember those books of yours, *In Search of Ancient 'Israel'* and *Scribes and Schools*, weren't they? Stirred up a few biblical scholars back then when they first came out."

"Those priestly scribes needed a story to justify their political ambitions," Davis said, "so they simply wrote an amazing story about a people and a state for which there is no evidence."

"It's one thing to say there's no evidence," Zephyr said, "but another to say it didn't exist."

"But the evidence we have – mainly archaeology – points to a very different picture," Davis said, wiping out his logical square in the dirt.

"But doesn't the biblical material reflect theories about state formation in the Ancient Near East?" Norm said.

"I know you argued that in your recent *The Politics of Ancient Israel*," Davis said, falling into the deeply ingrained scholarly habit of citing something, anything. "But isn't it the other way around: the biblical narrative unconsciously affects political thought about state formation?"

"Maybe, maybe..." Norm said.

"But you owe so much to Norm," Rick said. "You might not buy the Canaanite origins of Israel, but didn't Norm start this whole new phase of suspicion of the sources. They say something, but it's very different from the story they tell. They reflect the time when they were composed. You just have a different theory about when they were written. Norm sees them coming from tribal Israel, or at least some of them. You argue they are much later."

"Oh come on everyone," Zephyr said, throwing her hands in the air. "Aren't we still doing the old historical critical thing? We still argue endlessly about dates of composition! What's so new about this?"

Norm sipped on a mug of buttermilk. "I'm guilty," he said. "I am at heart a historical critic, but not in the old sense."

"What sense then?" Zephyr said.

"A social science sense!" Norm exclaimed, chomping down on a tomato. Try as he might to take the whole tomato in his mouth, he could not quite manage. He left his mouth slightly open and the seeds sprayed out over his lap and legs and all over Rick and Davis.

Mellowed by the tea, Rick threw himself back on the grass and pissed himself laughing. Well, his pants didn't feel warm and cosy and somewhat wet, but he did laugh a lot. Here was Rick Cowley, almost crying from his mirth and covered with tomato pulp and seeds.

Davis, jumpy as ever, jumped up. "Good shot Norm," he cried. "Now I'm covered in seed. Is this what multiplying your seed means?"

"But," Davis went on, "I'm never sure with you Norm. Who's in control here: historical criticism or the social sciences?"

"Do I have to choose?" Norm said.

"Yes, you do!" the others said in chorus.

"Oh, what a choice!" Norm cried. "But no, I'm not into antagonism. The social sciences and historical criticism enhance each other, bring out the best in each other."

"But you've really left out that whole bunch of literary or postmodern methods, or as I prefer, critical theory," Zephyr said

"Oh, I think they can join the group. The more the merrier, and I think we can all get along," Norm replied.

"That's just *so* you!" Zephyr said lovingly. "But don't you think it would be a tight fit?"

"Hey, but when everyone loves one another..." Davis said.

"That makes it worse," Rick observed. They all nodded wisely.

"It might be a tight fit," Norm restarted, "but I think historical, literary and social science approaches can all get into bed together – as I tried in my socio-literary introduction to the Hebrew Bible."

"Eeew," Zephyr said. "Let me just poke that image from my mind's eye."

"What image?" Norm was puzzled.

"All those biblical scholars in bed together, fitting things into tight places," Zephyr said. "Eeew," she said again and shook herself.

Rick crossed his legs, dropped his eyelids half-way and rocked slightly. He sang: "All you need is love, all you need is love."

"All you need is love, love, love is all you need," sang Norm as he joined in the old Beatles classic.

"I'm all for that," Davis said. "But you can't just say 'social sciences,' Norm, and leave it at that. What do you mean, what do you really mean by the social sciences?"

"Oh, you know," Norm answered, "sociology, anthropology, ethnography..."

"Not much progress, Norm," Davis said, "and what do they mean?"

"Well," Norm said, "if sociology begins with collective experience and moves to the individual, anthropology goes in the other direction, from individual to social."

"Pretty much the same, it seems to me," Davis said, "except maybe with different emphases. I bet they fiercely guard their finely defined territories."

"You can count on it," Norm said.

"How about this," Rick offered. "Let's say we spend a day observing people crossing a road with traffic. Sociologists will watch for repeated actions, ones that people will unconsciously repeat and then ask why they do so as a group – childhood training, picking up things from others, and so on. Anthropologists will look not so much for what is the same but for what is distinct. Why does this person behave this way, and that person in another? And then the anthropologist will look for reasons within society."

"Except that sociologists will go and observe people in their own, contemporary societies," Norm said, "while anthropologists have a liking for remote tribes or ancient peoples – any group that is far removed from her own: Margaret Mead in the Pacific Islands or Claude Lévi-Strauss in the highlands of Brazil."

"So," Davis said, "that would make you more of an anthropologist than a sociologist, Norm. Ancient Israel is hardly a modern society."

"Oh, how tame!" Zephyr said. "Nothing scandalous in that. So Norm is an anthropologist. Whoopee!"

"Yeah Norm," Rick said, "what about the M-word?"

Norm fell quiet. They waited for his response, but he had become shy.

"Uh," Davis said. "That's about as much organic food as I can handle! I reckon I've added five years to my life with this meal. Now for the balance." He leaned over and grasped the greasy bag and opened it out to a vast pile of potato chips and heavily battered and deep fried fish.

"Mmmm," he mumbled, a drooping piece of what may have been shark in one paw and a bunch of long chips in the other. "Anyone bring any grog?"

"Oh yes!" Zephyr cried. "I've got some organic elderberry wine here."

"Oh wow," Rick said, "and I've got some nettle beer."

"And here's some alcoholic apple juice," Norm added.

"Oh God!" Davis groaned. "Please help me! Well, I've got a bottle of cheap whisky. Anyone for a drink?"

The others screwed up their faces as one.

"That'll be the death of you," Zephyr said. 'You sure you don't want some elderberry wine? It'll do you a world of good."

"Nope," Davis replied, and poured out a mug of whisky.

"Cheers," he said. They shrugged at Davis' antics, believing he would be converted at some point. But they did say "cheers" in return.

"The M-word, Norm!" Davis said. "We all know you're a Marxist, an American Marxist. And if that wasn't enough of an oxymoron, you're a biblical American Marxist. Please tell me you're not from Texas, since that would be the ultimate, quadruple oxymoron."

"Sorry to disappoint you," Norm said. "But I do know someone who fits your exact description – Mark Sneed is a Texan American Marxist biblical scholar."

"But why in the world do you keep your discussion of Marx to the last section of that massive *Tribes of Yahweh* book?" Rick asked. "Why not put it out front?"

"It's not as though there was a pile of biblical Marxists back then in the seventies," Norm replied. "Didn't want to put people off. It was still the Cold War, we were shaking off McCarthy. I couldn't just say, hey, I'm a Marxist and here's my reading of the Bible."

"Yeah," Zephyr said, "and that was before Belo and Clevenot in Europe and their materialist readings, and liberation theology was only just stirring. Marx just wasn't on the lips of biblical scholars."

"Sure was on the lips of the New Left!" Rick said.

"So," Norm went on, "I wanted to let my biblical reading speak for itself without laying on the theory too thick."

"Fair enough, but what about Max Weber and Emile Durkheim on society and religion?" Rick asked. "When you get to the theory, you've some good slabs on them."

"Yeah, you sure get into the jargon, Norm," Zephyr said. "My favourite has to be 'religio-political servo-mechanism'!"

"That's a doozie!" Rick said, falling over sideways laughing.

"How about this one," Zephyr said, in between guffaws, " 'mono-Yahweh is a servo-mechanical feedback loop'!"

Norm was embarrassed. "I didn't write that," he said.

"No, but it's close," Rick laughed.

"OK," Norm said, "I might draw on Durkheim's theory that religion expresses the best of a community's hopes, that it has a positive role, and Weber on ideal types, but Marx lies beneath all of that," he said.

"You are a Marxist at heart, aren't you Norm?" Zephyr said.

"Quite simply," Norm replied. "Marxism provides the most comprehensive and sophisticated theory that links history, society, belief, thought, culture, politics..."

"Preaching to the converted, Norm, talking to the converted," Rick said.

"That cool dude sitting on his carbuncles in the British museum sure hit on something, for all his failings," said Davis. "I'm a Marxist too, you know, a heretical Marxist who just happens to like greasy fish and cheap whisky."

"I think we all would be," Zephyr said. "If I'd pursued my feminist Marxism in the old Eastern Bloc I would have been silenced."

"But it's true," Rick said, "we can't even imagine biblical studies without the social sciences now. You sure put a bomb under biblical studies and we felt it all the way across the Inter-Testamental period and into the New Testament. Now there's a wealth of books using the social sciences alone or in conjunction with other methods. There's research units and program units and reading groups, and any self-respecting introductory course in biblical studies must include the social sciences as a tried and true approach."

"Yeah, but what's the situation now?" Davis asked. "How do you sort the wheat out from the chaff, the sheep from the goats...?"

"Have you been reading your Bible again, Davis?" Rick teased him.

"Oh yeah," Davis said, "I do occasionally do that, but not last thing before I go to sleep for some uplifting passage about rape, slaughter and general divine mayhem."

"The situation now?" Zephyr said and sat thinking for a few moments.

"More tea anyone?" Norm asked.

"I'm good with this whisky," Davis said.

"And I'm in the middle of my elderberry wine," Zephyr added. "But you know what I think: there's two main areas where the social sciences are the best."

"Where?" Rick said.

"OK, we all admit there's precious little evidence available for the ancient Near East, let alone Palestine."

"But we've got much more than we had – there's a pile of archaeological data," Norm said.

"Yeah, but compare that with, say, how much material we have for the seven years of World War II," Zephyr said. "It's still possible for one person to know what has been discovered in the ancient Near East. Try that for World War II. And instead of seven years of history, our stuff concerns millennia. Try comparing all we have for the last two millennia with the two before that! They just don't compare in terms of the information we have available."

"So?" Davis said.

"It means we just have to use comparative material from other societies to help us see what Israel might have been like," Zephyr said.

"Right on!" Norm exclaimed. "That's why I've been doing some work with Icelandic society around 1000 CE."

"And then there was Evans-Pritchard's famous work with the Nuer in Africa," Rick said, "or the work on slave society in USA in the eighteenth and nineteenth centuries."

"Or the Awlad 'Ali Bedouin studied by Lile Abu-Lughod," added Zephyr, "or Mediterranean codes of shame and honour studied by Julien Pitt-Rivers, or James Scott's work on the subversive strategies of Malaysian peasants…"

"Enough, more than enough," Davis said, a wondering look under his bushy eyebrows. "There's a fair bit of that stuff, isn't there?"

"Gotta supplement our information somehow, especially if we're dealing with tribal societies," Norm said, "but we need to be careful."

"Why?" Davis asked.

"Oh, we can't just take data from contemporary Bedouin societies," Norm said, "and apply it to a society in the ancient Near East some three thousand years ago."

"That's assuming such a society existed," Davis reminded them. "Ignore the minimalists at your peril!"

"Oh yeah," Zephyr said, "I forgot. You minimalists think that ancient Israel never existed."

"Not quite," Davis said. "We think there was indeed something in those highlands in Judaea, but it sure as hell wasn't the Israel we read about in the Hebrew Bible. *That* is pure fiction. It has about as much historical worth as the book of Mormon and its stories about Moroni and Mormon before Europeans arrived in North America."

"We?" Rick was quizzical. "You said, '*we* think…'"

"Yeah," Davis replied, "me and Niels-Peter Lemche and Thomas Thompson and Keith Whitelam."

"Even so," Norm said, "we can still use comparative materials from the social sciences, but we need to be so sensitive to the differences as well as similarities. Ever since Lewis Henry Morgan's work on the gens among the Iroquois in the nineteenth century, there's been so much potential for biblical studies, so much that helps make sense of obscure texts – with Morgan it was the clan structure that shows through in the texts in all sorts of ways – but still we have to be very careful about those comparisons, no matter how useful they are."

"Right," Davis said. "Comparisons aside, I'm really interested in Marx. Forget Weber and Durkheim and social scientific comparisons, but what about Marx?" He leant back, took a deep draught from his mug of whisky and his shirt fell open. Beneath he wore a black T-shirt with the well-known icon of Karl on it. Bearded, grey, eyes twinkling, Karl gazed upon these hippies of the third millennium. Beneath the visage were the words, "Revolution, dude!" emblazoned in red.

"What about Marx?" Norm said.

"Well, I know I like my cheap whisky, and I know I drive an expensive car," Davis said, his grey buzz-cut standing on end, "but I want to know what Marx contributes to biblical studies – apart from mode of production."

"Some basic, indispensable, crucial categories," Norm said.

"Do you think you might have added foundational, significant, momentous, major and noteworthy?" Zephyr said in a moment of thesauric affirmation.

"I'd say basic, or maybe infrastructural," Rick said.

"That's it," Norm cried, leaning forward in his eagerness.

"What's it?" Davis said.

"Base," Norm said.

"As in…baseball," Rick said and smiled knowingly.

"No, no, no," Norm said, "as in base and superstructure. It's a basic" – they all groaned – "category in Marxism."

"So how does it work?" Davis asked.

"OK," Norm waxed strong. He felt his healthy lungs giving him strength, a really new feeling. "The superstructure includes things like culture and religion and politics and law and beliefs and the way people make sense of the way they live in the world – in other words, ideology…"

"Ideology?" Davis interrupted him.

"Ohhhh," Norm said, "that may well be one of the most debated questions within Marxism. I'm just going to come clean here. Ideology, especially in ancient Israel is

"the consensual religious ideas which were structurally embedded in and functionally correlated to the other social phenomena within the larger social system, and which served, in a more or less comprehensive manner, to provide explanations or interpretations of the distinctive social relations and historical experience of Israel and to define and energize the Israelite social system oppositionally or polemically over against other social systems" (TY: 66).

"What the *hell* does that mean, without all the social-science-speak?" Davis asked.

"Ideology is the imaginary relationship of individuals to their real conditions of existence," Norm said.

"But that's so close to Althusser it's not funny," Rick said. No one laughed – Althusser was, in general, not really a humorous fellow, having spent a few too many times in St. Anne's hospital for the mentally disturbed.

"Let me put it this way," Norm replied. "We believe we relate to the world in certain ways, but that belief is not the same as the actual relationship we have with that world. Ideology is the belief about that relationship, and may in fact have no connection to the actual relation. Ideology's always at one remove from the actual relationship we have with the world in which we live."

"What's the point of that gobbledygook?" Davis asked, yet again.

"OK," sighed Norm. "Let's take your priests who you say wrote most of the Hebrew Bible."

"Yeah, let's take them, the bastards," Davis said.

"Oh you're so much like Wellhausen it's not funny," Norm said. "But a crude version of ideology would see them as cynical manipulators of the tradition and the people. They construct a history of Israel – a purely fictional one, you say – in order to further their political ambitions."

"Yeah, and?"

"Well," Norm said, "that's so crude it's not funny."

"Crude I am," Davis said.

"Yeah but," Norm went on, "what's interesting here is not whether the priests were cynical manipulators or propagandists – that's a widespread and crude notion of ideology: they have their beliefs and they try to propagate them. What's far more interesting is *how* they see themselves. It's not that they are trying to put forward their beliefs, their ideology, but the fact that they *think*, that they *imagine* they are doing so. That imagination is ideology. And the same applies to your theory: how you see the priests shows forth your own ideology."

"I think I've got it," Davis said, thinking long and hard.

"Quite basically," Norm said, "we can't live without ideology – like the air we breathe. Ideology gives us a story about how we live in this world."

"Why didn't you say it like that in the *first* place!" Davis cried. "Talk about extracting blood from a stone."

"And then there's class..." Zephyr said.

Norm spouted forth yet again:

> "Class is seen to exist when some people live off the labor product of others. This living off the product of others is called *exploitation* in the objective sense that the value of one laborer's production, over and above the laborer's need for subsistence, is appropriated by someone else. This labor product beyond the subsistence need of the laborer is called *surplus product* which is also *surplus value* because the exploiter consumes or exchanges the *good* of the object produced thereby denying the producer the use or exchange of the object that embodies the producer's labor... Similarly, then, *class conflict* is... an objective description that producers and non-producers struggle to increase, diminish, or arrest the appropriation of surplus value" (HB: 147-48).

"Hold on, hold on! You theory-head!" Davis said, shaking his head. "Class, exploitation, surplus value, class conflict...?"

"Let me put it this way," Norm said, "a peasant works the land for crops, milks a cow or two for milk, shears a sheep for wool for garments for his family and associates. But then there's another group – the king's court, priests, scribes and others – who don't do these things, but they still need to live in some way. So they take some of the peasant's produce for food, clothing and so on. What they take is *surplus value*, although they usually take far more than they need and it usually means that the peasant struggles to survive. The technical term for this is *exploitation*. And the two groups – those who work and those who take from those who work – form *classes* that by definition are opposed to each other. So we have *class conflict*."

"Would the tithe extracted by the priests be an example?" Davis asked.

"Absolutely!" Norm replied.

"Brilliant theory," Rick said, "Here's to Marx!" They lifted their mugs with cries of "Ugly old bugger" and "To Steam Engine" and "To the Moor."

"Steam Engine? Moor?" Davis said.

"They're some of the names his daughters gave him," Zephyr said, "...he had a dark complexion. Along with Challey and Old Nick."

"Don't usually think of Marx as a tender dude who loved his daughters to death," Rick said. "Go figure..."

"Let's not get too sentimental!" Davis cried. "Now we're getting like all touchy-feely. You know, where we all get in touch with our inner selves, share our spiritual path, hold hands and pray for each other."

Rick shivered. "Uhhhh, sounds like a theological college I used to work in once."

"Yeah," Davis said, "you touch me, I'll feel you."

"Sounds like you, Davis! Here, give me some lovin'." Rick reached over and gave him a huge hug, smacking him loudly on the cheek in brotherly love.

Davis shook him off, and the others laughed while he said, "You sure can tell a New Testament critic – they'll give anyone the kiss of peace when they get the chance!"

"But Norm gave you the kiss of peace and he's Hebrew Bible," Zephyr said.

Davis ignored her. "OK," he said, "so you've got these Marxist ideas – mode of production, class and class conflict, ideology, exploitation, surplus value and so on – but do you then apply them like a recipe or, as the Americans are fond of calling it, a cookie cutter to the archaeological and literary data?"

"If you want to be vulgar about it," Rick said, burping loudly.

"Always liked Vulgar Marxists," Davis said, "I count myself as one. I'll be damned!" He paused in a profound moment of insight. "Why don't we call ourselves that – the Vulgar Marxists?"

"With an emphasis on vulgar or Marxist, Davis?" Zephyr said.

"Oh, you know me," Davis said.

"But we can't be too vulgar about our biblical work," Rick said.

"Why not?" Davis queried.

"All these ideas," Rick said, "the ones we've been discussing, they're really a bunch of problems that are worth working with rather than any recipe: you don't get Marxism by adding a tablespoon of class, half a cup of ideology, a cup of surplus value and then mix in mode of production. No, they're problems we need to think about, rework, maybe rename or discard, and maybe come up with a few new ones."

"That's all fine in theory," Davis said, "we can all sit around drinking organic hippie alcohol – God forbid – but what about politics?"

"Politics?" Rick asked.

"Yeah," Davis said, "isn't Marxism just as much about politics, political activity, a way of thinking about and acting in the world, apart from riding bicycles and eating the right food?"

"Sure," Zephyr said, "Marxism's one of those methods that comes out of a political passion – like feminism, like queer theory, like postcolonialism, like…"

"But what do you do about it, apart from interpret texts?" Davis insisted.

"I've been a member of the Democratic Socialists for years," Norm said.

"*What?*" Zephyr said, "I didn't know that Norm."

"I bet most biblical scholars don't know it either," Norm said. "It began way back in the fifties and the anti-nuclear protests that then fed into the Vietnam War protests in the sixties and seventies."

"Along with the whole civil rights movement in the southern USA," Rick added.

"And the social justice message of the prophets screamed to be heard at that time," Norm said. "How do you keep some sort of religious commitment and get into political activity? Well, it's all there in the prophetic protest against exploitation and oppression. So we drew on the prophets to hammer US foreign policy, domestic racism, the right to political speech critical of the US government and its militarized society."

"Nothing much has changed with the gangsters in power now," Rick said.

"No, the neo-cons really think the USA should have fought it out in Vietnam," Zephyr said. "Now they're saying that we, and the West in general (which for them was pretty much the same thing), would have been better off without the sixties. They're not silly, these neo-cons, since no sixties meant and means no women's liberation, no indigenous politics, no black power, no liberation theology, no new left, no rediscovery of Marx..."

"And we wouldn't be sitting here now if there hadn't been a sixties," Rick added.

"If we didn't have the sixties, we would have had to invent them!" Norm said.

"But," Zephyr said, "they didn't just happen spontaneously in the West – you know, the revolution of May '68 in France, the Prague spring, the turbulence in England, Europe, Australia. That's really arrogant, assuming the West produced all this by itself. Fred Jameson – now there's a tough read! – argues that all this happened as a response to the wars of anti-colonialism around the world. *Those* anti-colonial struggles produced the sixties!"

"Hmmm," Rick said, "Jameson's a cool dude too."

"But why Marx?" Davis said.

"Well, we were hearing a lot about Marx in the sixties," Norm said, "so along with the prophets I began to read Marx. The two seemed to be saying many of the same things! And it wasn't just me. The students began asking more and more what the connections were between the texts we were reading and the events we were reading about daily in the news and experiencing in our lives. Some took a policy of non-involvement, but for those of us involved, there were endless meetings, debates, protests and other action. And we had the whole range – pacifists, non-pacifists, anarchists, communists..."

"Hey," Zephyr, "sounds like the huge coalitions we now get in the anti-capitalist and anti-globalization protests, from Seattle to Melbourne to Madrid to Seoul..."

"It's really heart-warming to see that again," Norm said, "since for a while, in the greedy eighties, we thought all of that had faded away, that the sixties were long gone."

"And now we've got a whole new generation of teenagers getting radicalized," Rick added. "My grandkids pass around music by Rage Against the Machine, they think deeply about the world they're going to inherit."

"Yeah," Zephyr said, "and I hear that in countries with Green parties, like New Zealand, Australia and many European countries, their overwhelming vote comes from people under thirty."

'So,' Rick said, 'for you Marx made sense of life outside the lecture room and in the texts you were reading.'

"But also theoretically," Norm said,

> "among all the theorists I encountered, it seemed to me that Marx was offering an apparatus that was most relevant to the issues I was tackling in biblical studies. You know, his way of asking questions, his way of bringing together the usually separated social and political realities, was working for me... Marx provided the right questions for uncovering the systematic connections among economic, social and political forces, even if one didn't like all of his answers" (TTY: 160-61).

"Hey, but Norm," Zephyr said, "Do you think it was a youthful thing? You know, protests and rock concerts are OK when you're young and idealistic, but later you get cynical and resigned. Like Winston Churchill said, if you haven't been a socialist in your youth, then you're as boring as an old fart."

"Really, did he say that?" Rick asked.

"Well, not quite," Zephyr said, "but it's how I'd imagine him saying it. But, Norm, was it just a youthful rush of blood?"

"No way," Norm replied, "like I said, these days I'm a member of the Democratic Socialists of America in the Berkeley area."

"The DSAs," Rick said, "what do they do?"

"Lots of grassroots activism," Norm replied, "speaking truth to power, keeping the faith."

They sat there, serious and sober. Well, not quite sober since the various drinks were taking their toll. Even alcoholic apple juice will do that to you after a while, or nettle beer, or... But they were serious, deadly serious. Politics was a deadly serious business. So much so that Davis had dropped off. Lying back on the grass, mouth open, his snores shook the branches on the ancient tree above them, driving small furry animals and snakes from their burrows and holes. Graves began to open and the dead were seen walking around. Well, not quite... A bee came lazily close to his nose.

"Tea, anyone?" Rick asked in between Davis' death rattles.

Zephyr smiled. "Ohhhh yeees," she said and reached for the thermos.

"Davis," Rick said, "*Davis!*" He yelled, shaking Davis' leg.

"What the...?" Davis opened one eye.

"Tea," Rick said, "you want more tea?"

"Absolutely," Davis smiled too. Rick was already smiling, in fact hadn't stopped smiling. Even the thought of that tea was enough to make you smile.

"We must be getting old," Norm said, "getting excited about a cup of tea."

"But this is some tea," Zephyr said, "*some* tea!"

So they sat and sipped, grey heads (apart from Zephyr's) nodding in a circle on the grass beneath a massive ancient tree, which thankfully decided not to drop a branch or two on them. For in a moment they had become an ancient circle in the late afternoon sun, wizards perhaps, or shamans, or mellowed prophets with the fire yet burning, or biblical scholars for whom the politics of compassion still mattered.

Chapter 6

ON THE BEACH: THE BIBLE AND CULTURE COLLECTIVE AND THE POSTMODERN BIBLE

"Surf's up!" Davey Doling yelled, after he had found his glasses.

"Surf?" Georg Ukelele said, laughing while donning his trademark gangster cap over buzz-cut white hair. "Yeah sure, there's surf, huge pounding two centimetre waves, Davey…if, and it's a big *if*, you can actually find your your way *to* the water, what with all the piers and closed amusement parks and boarded up holiday villas. And there's one small problem: you'll have to brave water that's full of pollution and barely five degrees Celsius."

"And what would we do in surf anyway?" Lisbett Flagelli asked while pouring herself a cup of bitumen-thick coffee. She hated thin coffee with milk or sugar, knowing full well that this was a mark of character. She spoke on: "None of us lives near the beach, owns a surfboard, or even knows what boardshorts are!"

"Or what an aquabog is," Stefan Less observed, accepting a coffee from Lisbett while undoing his ponytail.

"Aquabog?" Gianna Weiss asked, being careful to avoid doing anything of note.

"Yeah," Stefan said, "you know, when you're in a wetsuit, on your board and out past the point and then you need to crap…voila, aquabog!"

"Uh Stefan!" Gianna said, "too much *infurrmayshun*! Aquabogs! My Lord!"

"But how do you wipe your bum, Stefan?" Tini Seedlin asked.

"Let not thy right hand know what thy left hand is doing," Stefan said, "even if you have sea water to use…"

"Uhuhuhuhu," Willy Cotton responded, "and that's definitely not in the eyes of the reader."

"And how do *you* know, Stefan," Gazza Horselover asked, dapper and neatly friendly. "There ain't much surfing in Ireland."

"Involuntary surfing, maybe," Stefan said, "speshly after Friday-night drinks... But no, my uncle was a surfie..."

"Fat lot of good that's going to do us then," Georg said. "They would have been amazing Christmas gatherings – your mother the beautician, your father the butcher, your uncle the surfie..."

They had come together from the four points of the compass, or at least some distance, to gather at Blackpool. They had had such a glorious time at that last meeting on the beach in California, the one where the photo was taken that had unfortunately *not* made its way onto the dustcover of *The Postmodern Bible*. The press had slipped up on that one and put a photo of an entirely different group on the dustcover instead. In *the* photo they had piled on top of one another in a moment of blissful collectivity. So they were hot for the beach once more, an exodus from their various snowbound inland cities.

"Whose idea was this?" Gianna said.

"Was what?" Georg said.

"To come here," Gianna said, "to bloody Blackpool."

"Oh no," Davey said, "that was me. But I thought I'd booked a spot on the Black Sea – one of those beautiful spots once frequented by communist party officials in Eastern Europe."

"Oh wonderful," Gianna said, "Blackpool instead of the Black Sea...and I thought you'd come upon some Shrangri-La, some secret wonder known only to a few."

"Yeah Davey," Lisbett said, "great choice: a house with gaps in the walls you can drive a truck through, buckets of rain thrown at us by a howling winter wind and as for a beach, well maybe we could find it somewhere..."

"Who's that?" Fritz cried. He had withdrawn from the argument and had been staring for some time through the window.

"Who?" Georg said.

"There's a bunch of people down on the pier," Fritz said.

They all rushed to the window.

"What are they carrying?" Willy asked.

"Planks of wood?" suggested Davey.

"Nah," Tini said, "they're airbeds."

"Don't be ridiculous," Georg said, "they're surfboards."

"You're kidding," Gianna said, "who in their right minds would bring surfboards to Blackpool?"

"Who said they were in their right minds?" Georg pointed out.

"Hey!" Fritz called. "*Hey you!*" He had opened the door while the others gaped out of the window. A blast of cold air made the rest collectively shiver and yell out to close the friggin' door. Fritz stood at the front step, waving and yelling at the three bedraggled figures down by the wharves.

As they drew close he asked, "Are you lost?"

"Yeah," said a tall, curly-haired man, "we're looking for the Bible and Culture collective."

"You ain't lost," Fritz said, "we're it."

"What? *Here*?" said the woman, tall and blond with a delicious northern English accent.

"Yep, you got it," Fritz said.

"What are you doing in Blackpool?" asked a second man. He too was tall and somewhat blond, although some would have said straw-coloured, as indeed many did from time to time.

"What's with the boards?" Fritz asked.

"Oh, we thought there might be some surf here," said the first man.

"Yeah, surf, sand and sex," the woman said.

"Don't you mean surf, sun and socialism?" the second man asked.

"Well, there's no sand, precious little sun, and a definite struggle for socialism," Fritz said. "Not sure about the sex though. But come in, come in."

"No hurry," said the woman, "we quite like driving winter rain."

They laughed and stepped over the threshold, shaking themselves like dogs, propping surfboards in the corner. Their hosts watched them, silent, open-mouthed like those fish that sweep the ocean floor.

"The Bible and Culture Collective," Fritz said, waving his arm in the direction of his comrades "but I'm sorry," he turned to the three figures, "I didn't catch your names."

"Geraldo East," the first man said, "from North Africa."

"Ivy Forest," said the woman, "and I'm from Ireland."

"And I'm Ronald Wildham," the last of them said. "I'm from…"

At that moment Fritz coughed and Ronald's location was lost on them all. But Fritz pondered whether they always spoke in sequence.

"Hello," the collective said with one voice.

"What the…?" Ivy cried.

"Are you guys, like, a choir?" Ronald asked.

"No," the collective said, "we speak as one."

"But you're individuals!" Geraldo cried.

"Yes," the collective said, "we're individuals."

"So why speak as one?" Geraldo asked.

"Because," they said, "we wrote *The Postmodern Bible* together – there's no individual section in it."

"Do you do this all the time?" Ronald asked. "Speak together, I mean. Do you do this when you're together alone?"

"Oh yes!" The collective said. Fritz raised his eyebrows.

"Fantastic!" Geraldo said. The collective smiled a collective smile. "Then you'll be able to answer our questions so much more easily."

"Questions?" The collective said.

"Questions indeed," Ivy said, "we have loads of them, like how the hell are we supposed to surf around here?"

"Oh, you could try putting a sail on your boards," suggested the collective, "and jump from the wharves. There's plenty of wind."

"Bugger that," Ronald said.

"Bugger what?" asked the collective.

"Bugger *you!*"

"Ohhhhhhhh," sighed the collective.

"Look," said Geraldo, "do you people have any beer?"

"Do we have beer?" The collective asked, "do we have *beer*? Of course we have beer. Sit down, sit down, we'll get some." The collective crowded into the kitchen, all trying to get to the fridge for the beer…except for Davey. He broke from the group and picked up a few bottles standing on the floor. And while the rest of the collective gradually sorted out how to remove beer from the fridge, Davey returned to the lounge room with his loot. He handed a beer to Ivy, Geraldo and Ronald, dropped on the lounge and opened his own.

Ronald took a swig from his bottle: "This beer's *warm*!" He cried.

Before Davey could respond – he would have said that the only drinkable beer is one that could be drunk at room temperature – well, before Davey could respond the collective returned with a stack of beer.

"Wow!" Ivy said, "there sure are some advantages to doing things collectively!"

The collective circled the coffee table and then as one smothered it with a mountain of beer. They joined Davey on the lounge – obviously a rather long lounge, a stretch limo of a lounge in fact. It was a bit of a squash, but a few sat on the laps of others and they all became more comfortable.

"Do you think it's worth it?" Ronald asked as they cracked open some cold ones.

"What?" The collective said, "sitting on the lounge together?"

"*No!*" Ronald shot back. "This collective experiment I mean."

"Yes," said Davey and Georg.

"Not at all," Gianna said.

"What?" Ivy cried. "I thought you always spoke as one."

"Not really," Gianna said.

"It's actually a little tricky," Davey said. "It's hard work."

"You can say that again," Ivy laughed.

"But it's really hard to know what a collective really is," said Tini.

"What do you mean?" Ronald asked.

"We usually start from individuals and ask how we might gather together," Tini said, "but how do you begin from a collective identity and then think of individuals in that light?"

"I wonder," Davey added, "whether we still really don't know what a collective is, whether we'll only know at some future, qualitatively different time. That's why our effort looks so clumsy a lot of the time."

"You've been reading too much Jameson, Davey," Tini teased.

"Yeah maybe," Davey replied, "but it's worth a go all the same."

"Why?" Geraldo asked.

"It's political," Tini said. "At some level or other we are all pinkos, some a shade closer to red. The struggle to make this work as a collective is part of that."

"And we also set out to oppose the a-political piece of tripe Robert Alter and Frank Kermode put out," Stefan said.

"You mean *The Literary Guide to the Bible*," Ivy said.

"Yeah," Stefan said, "they just assume that we begin reading as individual aesthetes. A new version of New Criticism, really, where you exclude all those annoying issues such as feminism, Marxism, biography, politics, ideology, psychoanalyis and so on and just read the text…"

They all laughed long and hard.

"And then they all come sneaking in the back door anyway," Ivy said.

"Yeah, along with the gays," Ronald said.

"OK," Geraldo said, giving Ronald a dirty look, "but the book made a splash when it came out. It still is a basic text for many who want to get a good introduction to the whole range of methods of reading that are around these days."

"We even went to the Modern Language Association meeting soon after it came out to run a panel there," Georg said. He had been speaking around Lisbett's back, for they were still seated on the limo of a lounge, and Lisbett was still upon his lap.

"I think I might get up," Lisbett said.

"No hurry," said Georg. "Didn't want that leg anyway!"

Lisbett wondered off to the kitchen, looking for a bottle of wine. Beer's not really my thing, she thought to herself, digging around for a bottle opener. Nor, for that matter, are old, decrepit wharf worker's houses. Not quite the beach house she had imagined.

"But why did you choose the methods you did?" Ivy asked. "Let me see...you deal with reader-response, structuralism, narratology, poststructuralism, rhetorical criticism, psychoanalysis, feminism, womanism and ideological criticism... A curious bunch, don't you think?"

"Curious?" Gazza asked.

"Well," Ivy went on, "some are not particularly new, like reader-response, structuralism, rhetorical criticism... Even feminism isn't necessarily what you'd think of as postmodern."

"It's a bit of a snapshot as to what was happening in the early nineties," Gazza said.

"And what interested us as well," Fritz said.

"What we were trying to do," Gazza said, "was pick up both newer and important currents in biblical studies at the time *and* point to others in literary criticism that needed much greater attention in biblical studies."

"Does that explain reader-response?" Geraldo said.

"Yeah, that one really was the pressure-chamber for biblical critics first discovering that there was more than just historical criticism," Fritz said.

"And for a while," Lisbett added, "people thought reader-response really *was* postmodernism. You know, meaning becomes something the reader brings to the text rather than what the author intended."

"It did help people see that there was something outside authorial intention," Georg said, "but it sure doesn't get you very far."

"At least it helps you see why there are so many interpretations of a text," Lisbett said. "You know, why for instance the story of the Exodus can provide inspiration for struggles for liberation and it can be used for the most conservative positions."

"And rhetorical criticism?" Ronald asked.

"An oldie and a newie," Willy said, leaning forward. "I've dabbled in this now and then. Thing is, there's a long German tradition of rhetoric that both goes way back into the past and faces a complete overhaul in the present."

"Am I right in thinking that it is pretty much a New Testament phenomenon?" Ronald asked.

"Probably now," Willy said, "but it started with James Muilenburg's famous address at the Society of Biblical Literature in 1968. He called for close attention to literary structure and coherence and sparked off a whole series of rhetorical studies. And then there's always Phyllis Trible who claims to be doing rhetorical analysis."

"Depends what you mean by rhetorical analysis," Bob Chick said. "If it's in the strict sense – you know, a set of accepted practices and rules for persuading an audience – then it is much more a New Testament thing, especially since the idea of rhetoric comes so much from ancient Greece. But if you give a somewhat looser sense, as in maybe attention to the small details of a text, then maybe Trible would fit. But she throws in reader-response and feminism too."

"But doesn't Robert Alter do that?" Ivy said, "you know, look for signs of composite artistry that ends up persuading the reader to the narrator's position?"

"Yeah, and Meir Sternberg a few years back with the whole Tel Aviv school," Geraldo said.

"A souped-up version of New Criticism maybe?" Ivy pondered. "A close reading of a text, watching for the minute variations in words, the way they come together in phrases and senses..."

"But it's still so a-political," Tini insisted.

"That's the legacy of New Criticism," Ronald said, "and it sure suits places like the USA that so often tend to have obnoxious internal and foreign polices. It's so easy to say: Oh, we won't bother with grubby politics and we'll just get on with reading our texts."

"But rhetoric *is* political," Willy said. "After all it's about persuading an audience, moving them, and that's political. Isn't that central to political speeches and political writing?"

"It's also central to biblical texts, if not more than other types of rhetoric." Davey said. "There are endless speeches and stories that work this way. The problem is that it's so often reactionary and obnoxious. There's Joshua's fictional speech on his deathbed, the justification for the conquest of Canaan, the denigration of the Jews in the New Testament..."

"But aren't we getting back to authorial intention?" Georg said.

"I guess so," Willy said, "except that the effect of a text is so often not what the author expects. The text's effort at persuasion goes awry and ends up in all sorts of directions."

"*I'd* like to persuade you to have a glass of wine," Lisbett said, coming back from the kitchen.

"I'm good with this beer," Ronald said.

"That sure worked!" Lisbett said.

"Wine?" Willy said. "Lovely!"

"Ah, now *that* worked!" Ivy said. "Just like water from the rock."

"And all I had to do was stand here with a bottle of wine and a glass and ask," Lisbett said. "I didn't even need to say it's fantastic wine."

"Would you find anything other than the best wine?" Willy asked.

"You know me," Lisbett said.

Deep in thought, Ivy had missed the wine talk. "You have a fascinating chapter on feminism," she said. "While celebrating the diversity and multiplicity of feminism, you really bring the question of race to the fore."

"What do you mean?" Tini asked.

"The feminist-womanist debate," Ivy said. "Womanism challenges feminism as white, middle class, wealthy. It points out that race is crucial, that 'women' is not a uniform category, that both men and women are included in and excluded from power, that class is central too. And all of this has a profound effect on the way you read and interpret the Bible. So, for instance, you don't see that Miriam's white skin – you know, when she is stricken with leprosy for questioning Moses in Numbers 12 – is a curse. And if you look at some of the older feminist work, it's so true – you know, Phyllis Trible, Elizabeth Schüssler Fiorenza, Mary Daly, Rosemary Radford Ruether..."

"But the context of the debate is crucial," Geraldo said, "and that's its real strength. This kind of debate could only have come out of the United States' long history of African slavery and the deep problems that race still presents the United States. What I'm trying to say is that where you have a history of slavery of a minority by a majority it sharpens the question of race in a particular way."

"It shows up today," Tini said, "in the way class and race are so often confused in the United States. For historical reasons most African Americans, as well Hispanics and Latinos, belong to the working class – usually the lower end of the working class. They do the jobs the whites don't want to do. But then their low socioeconomic status is seen by many to be a result of being African American, Hispanic and Latino, rather than the result of class dynamics."

"That's a classic Nazi argument!" Geraldo said. "You notice some cultural attribute and then give an ethnic reason for it. Who hasn't heard comments like: Africans are lazy, the Dutch are stingy, the English don't wash, Bulgarians are lazy, Poles don't know how to take care of their machinery, Germans are domineering, Chinese are shifty, Americans are loud and obnoxious...? And before you know it you have Nazi-style racism."

"What about the French?" Lisbett asked.

"What about them?" Geraldo said.

"I mean Irigaray and Kristeva," Lisbett said, "since they're in that chapter on feminism as well."

"What's their main point?" Geraldo asked. "Why are they in there?"

"They bring a very different edge to feminism," Davey said, "and it lies in the connections between psychoanalysis and feminism? And aren't both of them practising psychoanalysts?"

"And isn't Kristeva's point, or at least one of them," Tini added, "the repression of the maternal body?"

"Irigaray follows a similar line," Lisbett said, "at least initially."

"What?" Ivy cried. "We've got to get in touch with our mothers?"

"Not quite," Davey said, "they argue that the maternal body has been and is repressed. For Kristeva, this means focusing on the pre-Oedipal mother-child relationship, the moment before language and articulation, before Lacan's Symbolic. She calls this the semiotic and suggests that here we find real creativity, real poetry and holiness and madness."

"Hold on, *hold on!*" Ronald yelled. "Pre-Oedipal, symbolic, semiotic? What's all this gobbledygook?"

Davey sighed at Ronald's slowness. "Oedipus, my dear Ronald, killed his father and slept with his mother in the Greek myth. So Freud took it as a story about the way a child grows up – the child metaphorically must replace his father in order to become an adult. For Lacan this becomes the crucial process into language and society – his is the realm Lacan calls the Symbolic. Without this Oedipal process you end up in psychosis. Kristeva uses 'semiotic' to describe the time before the Oedipus complex, when the relationship is only between mother and child."

"But what's all *that* got to do with the Bible?" Geraldo asked.

Davey continued patiently, "Kristeva's one of those big topic writers. She goes for the huge questions, like melancholy, or love, or nationhood, or the abject, and then sweeps across ancient Greece, the Bible, Western literature, philosophy, with sample readings from here and there. So she's written about the Bible, especially on the Madonna and child, and on the food taboo laws in Leviticus 11."

"Doesn't such a grand scheme threaten to be a bit thin at times?" Ronald asked.

"She writes with a deft pen," Davey said, "but yes, it can get superficial."

"Still," Geraldo said, "what would a Kristevan reading look like? And not Kristeva herself on the maternal body of Mary and the child, or the abject or whatever."

"Let me see..." said Davey. "Let's look at the Exodus. Kristeva is a strict Lacanian – there is no such thing as woman, woman cannot be represented – so we won't find it clearly in the text. It will be repressed in some way and only show up at all in its margins."

"So where is it then?" Ronald asked.

"In Canaan!" Davey said. "The land flowing with milk and honey is in fact the maternal body and Israel's relationship to it is the repressed mother-child relationship. It's thrown into the future, something desired, something for which the people wait endlessly, and then they are afraid of it when they get there."

"But doesn't Egypt function in a similar way?" Ronald asked.

"Yes of course!" Davey said. "Israel is born out of Egypt and then longs for it when they are in the desert. It too is called a land flowing with milk and honey in Numbers 16:13 and the people constantly mumble and grumble when they have left Egypt."

"So Egypt and Canaan merge into one," Geraldo said, "two ways the maternal body and the mother-child relationship are repressed in the story."

"Quick, give me another drink!" Ivy cried. "This Exodus story has got so many layers its making my head spin."

"You don't think," Georg said, "it might be the alcohol?"

"Never," Ivy said, "never!" She disappeared into the kitchen.

"OK," Ronald intervened. "What about Irigaray then?"

"She takes all of this a step further," Tini said, "and argues that it's not just the mother-child relationship that is repressed, but the mother-daughter relationship. Girls go through the whole process quite differently from boys. Kristeva blurs the two – her essay on the Virgin Mary is talking about a mother-boy relationship – while Irigaray wants to keep them quite separate."

"But isn't that because Irigaray's main point," said Lisbett, "is the idea of sexual difference. She argues – wrongly I think – that the real challenge is heterosexuality. According to her, we haven't so much as glimpsed a true heterosexuality; what we get is merely the dominance of men, and women become exchange objects between men."

"What about gays and lesbians then?" Ronald asked.

"Oh for Irigaray they just belong to the economy of the same," Lisbett said, "which is what we have anyway."

"But if we follow the idea of sexual difference through, wouldn't that mean the development of two different realms of men and women?" Geraldo asked.

"*That's* her big project," Lisbett said, "Irigaray is hot on the idea of two separate legal systems, two social systems, two cultures and two types of religion."

"Yeah, yeah," Ronald said, "but what does all that mean for the Bible?"

"Well," Davey came in, "now we can start to focus on moments in stories – almost forgotten – where women are on their own. It happens in Genesis 34. Dinah went out to see the daughters of the land, it says. Just a glimpse, but enough of something that is closed down."

"And then there's Jephthah's daughter in Judges 11," Tini added, "who before she is to be sacrificed goes off into the mountains with her female companions."

"So in the end," Ivy said peaking out from behind the kitchen door, "a reading inspired by Kristeva and Irigaray would not look to recover biblical women, but look for the almost complete repression of other things – like the maternal body or the mother-daughter relationship."

"Yes, but they do draw their key categories from Freud and Lacan," Davey said.

"Like what?" Ronald said.

"Well, like the Oedipus complex," Davey said patiently, becoming accustomed to Ronald's obtuseness. "And the return of the repressed, and the Symbolic and the Real..."

"There you go again," Ronald said. "We've had Oedipus and we've had the Symbolic, but the return of the repressed, and the Real?"

Davey sighed, again. "The return of the repressed is Freud's idea. When we repress something it shows up in all sorts of other ways, in the way we put our words together, in the way we act and think and dream. But it doesn't actually show up itself."

"So if, for instance," Ronald said, "I repress the memory of some horrible experience, like losing a teddy bear when I was a child, then it will show up how?"

"Well, you might get anxious about losing things," Davey said, "or you might become obsessive about hanging onto things and people that are dear to you."

"But the Bible?" Ronald asked.

"Freud, the crafty bugger," Davey said, "actually got many of his categories from the Bible. So he argued that God is in fact a sign of the repression of the murder of the father, of the leader of the Israelites."

"You mean Moses?" Ronald said.

"Yeah, that's him," Davey said. "The Israelites murdered him, and then to repress the memory they elevated him into a divine figure full of anger and jealousy and so on."

"What bull!" Ronald said. "That psychoanalysis really is a crock of..."

"The murder of the father is one of the great myths of psychoanalysis," Davey said, "especially in the way Freud argues it in *Moses and Monotheism*.

But we can track the return of the repressed all over the place – you know, for instance, Christianity represses its Jewish roots and that shows up in anti-Semitism."

"And the Real?" Ronald asked.

"Well that's Lacan's take on all of this," Davey said. "The Real isn't reality, it's what can't be represented or named and yet it affects everything. A bit like the moon below the horizon that affects the tides."

"Not bad," Ronald said, "not bad at all."

"No but it goes further," Davey said, "since the Real is actually what keeps everything together – ourselves, society and so on. It's precisely what is excluded that is the glue of our fragile lives. If it does show up, then everything would fall to pieces."

"Hey," Geraldo said, "isn't that a bit like Kristeva's abject?"

"Sure is," Davey replied, "except that Kristeva develops it from Lacan."

"So what *does* belong to the Real?" Ronald asked.

"God for one," Davey replied, "and woman."

"So in the wanderings in the wilderness," Geraldo said, "God is what you might call an absent cause, the moon below the horizon, and that's why you can't name him or represent him, and he appears in clouds of smoke and fire. And he's the one that knits the narrative together."

"Oh my God!" Ronald said, "I've lost my diary!" He stood up and bent over to look behind the lounge. As he had put on a bit of weight and become a bit of a porker, his pants split along his bum crack. Everyone but Ronald pissed themselves laughing.

"You're falling to pieces, Ronald!" Georg said. "Careful, or you'll lose your identity entirely."

"Speaking of which," Ivy said, feeling slightly rough at the edges, "what about autobiographical criticism. There's none of that in *The Postmodern Bible*."

"Maybe that's because it hardly existed then," Stefan said. "Well, it did outside biblical studies, but had been around only for a few years. It all began with Jane Tompkins' essay 'Me and my Shadow' from 1987. She weaves her theoretical reflections in with a very personal narrative about sitting in socks on a cool evening, feeling like a piss but not going yet. Since then autobiographical criticism has crept in on the edges of a number of other approaches. Obviously feminism, but also cultural studies, some postcolonial criticism, anthropology and so on."

"But what's the point?" Ronald objected. "Isn't autobiography a really tricky zone?"

"I think it's a deep reaction against the false objectivity of a so-called 'scientific' biblical studies," Stefan said, "let alone other disciplines. And I *really* like it."

"Let's not get too personal," Tini said. "But I do like it. When it's good, it's *good*. I still think the best example is Jeff Staley's *Reading with a Passion*. He brings his life as the pastor's son on an Indian reservation into contact with the Gospel of John."

"But," Geraldo said, "autobiography would have to be one of the most complex forms of fiction. If someone can write four or five autobiographies, each quite different from the other, then it becomes a little suspicious."

"But don't you think it's a refreshing change?" Stefan said.

"Of course," Geraldo said. "I love reading it, but when it becomes the basis for some unquestionable moment of authenticity I have a lot of trouble. Much of it says: this is my experience, and from this experience I'm writing this. This is *me*! You haven't had this experience, so you can't challenge it."

"So the search for authenticity really should be questioned?" Stefan asked.

"Or rather," Geraldo said, "the best autobiographies are those that are consciously fictional and playful – like Louis Althusser's *The Future Lasts a Long Time*. The problem is that if you write autobiographically, readers somehow assume you really are writing about yourself."

"So what's a good autobiographical take on the Exodus then?" Ronald asked.

"You'd have to avoid using autobiography as a glue to keep your argument together," Stefan said as a cushion came unstuck from the lounge. "You know, like the story of the Golden Calf that you want to read in terms of dairy farming, and you tie it all together with a story about your childhood on a dairy farm. And God forbid that you'd authenticate your reading through autobiography – such as basing your reading of alcohol in the Bible on your experience of brewing beer. The ones I like best are when you might track the role of certain texts at key points in a fictional autobiography – for instance, the law about killing rowdy and disobedient teenagers at the gate of the city and your experience of this text as a teenager with fundamentalist parents."

Only Stefan laughed.

Ivy, however, returned from the kitchen, did an about-face as she forgot something and then came back again. "Let's get back to the book," she said. "What about structuralism? Why's that in there? In fact, what *is* structuralism?"

"Structuralism," Davey said slowly and quietly, leaning back in his chair "is a general theory of the intelligibility of mind based on the view that what makes things intelligible is their perceived relatedness, rather than their qualities as separate items."

"Oh Davey," Ivy cried. "You can do better than that!"

"How about this," Davey replied. "Our minds work with a very basic set of terms or concepts – lost and found, raw and cooked, plenty and scarcity and so on – and these concepts turn up in what we write or draw or paint or sculpt or build. So with the Exodus story we might read that long narrative in terms of scarcity and plenty. The wilderness is in fact a zone of scarcity that is answered by its opposite, plenty, in the land flowing with milk and honey."

"Speaking of which," Ronald said, "I'm suffering from a scarcity of beer. Any good porters here?" He rummaged around the bottles on the table and finally found a dark ale. "Ah, this will do!"

"Sounds all pretty basic," Ivy said.

"Oh, but then it becomes fun," Georg said, "since we need to distinguish between the high and low structuralists. Davey's definition of structuralism is a bit misleading, since he was talking about the high structuralists – they go for the deep structures, the small number of universal terms and oppositions that we can find in the huge variety of biblical texts. But there's also the low or surface structuralists, who take their cue from people like Validimir Propp and his work on the Russian folktale. They prefer to deal with the terms that appear more obviously in the text rather than some deep structures that the text points to."

"OK, I'm getting this," Ronald said, twisting the top of the beer bottle with his hand and squashing the lid between his thumb and index finger in a petty show of strength.

"Poser," Ivy said.

"Never!" Ronald said.

"So," Ivy said, "if a high structuralist reading of the Exodus focuses on the opposition of scarcity and plenty, what about a low structuralist interpretation?"

"Well," Davey said. "We might understand the wilderness as a lack, here a lack of milk and honey. Something, an act of 'villainy', has happened to bring about this lack, and that's Pharaoh's act of letting the Israelites go. Although here Yahweh has had a hand in it too – Pharaoh and Yahweh are collaborators at this point! Then there is the finding and equipping of a hero. It might be Israel itself, or more likely Moses and then Joshua – the hero can be more than one character. The hero then overcomes the lack – in this case of milk and honey – by getting the people into the land."

"It's not that different from the high structuralist opposition of scarcity and plenty," Roland observed.

"True," Davey said. "The distinction between high and low is a bit artificial. But there are two things I really like about structuralism. First, it's a deductive approach. The terms don't arrive from within a close reading of a short piece of text – that's *so* New Criticism! – but from a previous set of ideas that you explore in the text. You can then look at larger stretches of text to find patterns. And secondly I really like the idea of *actant*. The big difference from character is that more than one character might fill the role of actant. So in the story of the Exodus from Egypt, we find that Moses, Joshua and even Israel can fill the one role of hero."

"But isn't structuralism a bit old hat, as my father used to say?" Ivy asked. "I mean, weren't the founders of structuralism – Ferdinand de Saussure and Claude Lévi-Strauss and Charles Sanders Peirce and Vladimir Propp – working in the first half of the twentieth century? Didn't structuralism wane in the 1980s in literary studies and biblical studies? So why's it in the book?"

"And it's not particularly postmodern either," Ronald added. "Just a little too universal for that."

"Because Davey really likes it still, in some way," said Georg.

"And because Lévi-Strauss is really, really smart and sexy," Davey said.

There was a collective raising of eyebrows.

"Sexy?" Lisbett quizzed. "Whatever does it for you, I guess."

"Oh but don't forget that structuralism was really the seed-bed of so much new stuff in biblical studies," Stefan said. "After its explosion in the seventies, it gave energy to so many things. Now they're called literary approaches, or postmodern, or what I'd like to call critical theory."

"Yeah, and now historical critics need to take pot shots at us," Georg said, "calling us cute, or entertaining."

"Or ephemeral, or our readings fluff," added Gazza.

"Shows that we're a force to be reckoned with," Georg smiled, "even if we are a bit fluffy. I quite like fluff in the right places..."

"I wonder whether it's also because structuralism was at the intellectual centre of the revolts of May '68 in France," Ivy said.

"What?" Fritz asked.

"Wasn't," Ivy said, "one of the slogans painted on the walls of Paris, 'Structuralism doesn't walk on the streets.' Students at the barricades couldn't see how it affected their lives, their politics."

"Your point is?" Lisbett pushed.

"It's simple," Ivy said, "structuralism is what poststructuralism revolted against. We can't understand Derrida, Foucault and all the rest of that motley crew without structuralism."

"And I thought we could never understand Derrida without his coiffed, sly pose, atrocious dress sense and pipe," Ronald said.

"Or Foucault without his leathers, bath houses and S&M," Geraldo added.

"Or the extraordinary career move of dying of AIDS before the last volume of *The History of Sexuality* was ready for the press," Ronald said.

"A bit like Jesus, really," Stefan said, "good career move!"

"OK," Ronald said, "let's do a Jesus on deconstruction and pin it down. And KISS me!"

As Ronald desperately fought off a roomful of people trying to kiss him, he yelled, "No, no! Keep it simple stupid!"

"Oh, sorry!" Stefan said. "Deconstruction is 'a dismantling of structures (philosophical, cultural, political, institutional, and above all and from the start textual) that was designed to show how they were put together in the first place' (PMB: 120)."

"Hey, I can understand that," Ronald said.

"So what you do," Stefan went on, "is find what a text excludes. Usually a text or a system of thought or a social system gives us an illusion of coherence by excluding something. So you find the point where that system fails and use it as a lever to deconstruct – that is, show how a system keeps the false impression of coherence."

"So then," Ivy said, "all those narrative breaks and contradictions in the Exodus story are signs of a failed effort at coherence."

"Like the confusion at Sinai over who sees and hears Yahweh," Ronald said, "or how many times Moses ascends the mountain and with whom. So these aren't so much signs of the combinations of different sources, but the signs of an unstable coherence."

"And it's not for nothing that it happens with the story of the giving of the law," Davey said, "since the law is one of the major efforts at cohesion. If the text breaks down where the law is given, then it's a sign that this effort at cohesion – the law – is in trouble."

"And what about the idea of Israel?" Ivy said. "The text works overtime to give us an idea of an ethnically distinct Israel, but then it keeps slipping up and showing how polymorphous, how *un*distinct and mixed that idea of Israel really is in this text. In fact, it's precisely all those excluded peoples that turn out to be the basis of Israel. It is, in other words, the name for an extraordinary mix of peoples."

"But," Gazza said, "the catch is that deconstruction isn't a method, it's not something you apply to a text. It is a whole range of things, but in the end it really means that you just read very carefully."

"Oh, come on," said Ronald. "You're just kidding yourself! Isn't that position based on the apparent exclusion of method? In other words, doesn't the denial of method rely on method?"

"If we were going to apply Derrida to himself, I guess so," Gazza said.

"OK," Ivy said, with an ironic grin, "if Derrida's contribution is to show how what looks like it is coherent is actually based on excluding what is incoherent, then what about Foucault?"

"KISS me!" Ronald said. Much to his relief no-one jumped up.

"Foucault changed over time," Lisbett said, "but his basic point is that 'discourses of knowledge conspire to produce that which they purport to describe' (PMB: 139)."

"What?" Ronald said, "*what?*"

"Let's take an example," Lisbett said. "What about the prison? What do you think the function of the prison is?"

"To deal with criminals?" Ronald said.

"No," Lisbett cried triumphantly. "The prison creates the category of criminal. It's not a response but part of the definition of who a criminal is. The same applies to other things Foucault studied, like the mental institution and the creation of madness, medicine and production of illness and so on. And all of these developed in very specific ways in order to define what it means to be law-abiding, normal, healthy..."

"So then," Geraldo said, "biblical studies, especially its historical-critical version, thinks it is getting ever closer to the real Israel or the real Jesus or the real early Church, but it actually creates the objects it thinks it is studying."

"Aren't we doing the same thing as the text itself?" Roland said. "In the same way that the story of the Exodus creates a certain image of Israel – or rather many images of Israel – so also biblical scholarship creates its images of Israel."

"So," Ivy said, "all those histories of Israel, all that work to understand the history of the text and of its context, all that archaeology – they are all part of this construction of 'Israel' and its texts."

"But wasn't Foucault also interested in power?" Geraldo said. "It's what I like about Foucault, since he becomes much more useful for politics."

"Yes," Lisbett said, "especially micro-power or capillary power."

"What, power in your veins?" Ronald cried.

"No, in your capillaries, stupid!" Lisbett shot back. "But that's the point. He's interested in how power runs in all sorts of places. It's not monolithic at all. There's no simple equation of those with power and those without. Power isn't static. No-one just holds power, since it's constantly rearranging itself: the gaoler and prisoner both exercise power over each other."

"But doesn't that undermine any politics of opposition," Ronald asked, "since oppositional power will be part of existing power relations, will even be generated by them?"

"You'd think so, wouldn't you?" Stefan said, "but Foucault's work has been taken up and developed by a whole range of political movements, especially lesbigay politics."

"Lesbigay?" Ronald said.

Stefan copied Davey's sigh and said slowly. "Lesbian, bisexual and gay."

"But that's another noticeable absence in the book," Geraldo said.

"There's quite a bunch," Georg admitted, "like the New Historicism inspired by Foucault, or postcolonialism, or ecocriticism, or disability studies, or autobiographical criticism or ethology."

"Ethology?" Ronald queried, again.

"The study of animal behaviour, apparently," Georg said, "there was an article on the Syrophoenician woman in Mark 7, reading from the perspective of the dogs, in that newish journal *The Bible and Critical Theory*. Ethology is a sort of critical socio-biologism."

At that moment, Gazza appeared from the kitchen with a large bowl of fried somethings – it was not entirely clear what. To the forest of quizzical eyebrows he said, "Fried chicken livers!"

"I forgot how hungry I was," Georg cried.

"Mmmmm…" said Tini with a chicken liver already crushed between her teeth.

"I'll pass," Ronald said.

"Anything else on the way?" Fritz asked.

"Oh, just some dogs' dicks, sheep brains and whale blubber salad," Gazza said.

"Uhuhuhuhu!" Ivy uttered. "I'll eat anything once, but whale blubber salad?"

"A delicacy from Greenland," Gazza said.

"Dog's dicks?" Geraldo asked.

"French hotdogs, apparently," Stefan said. "Have you ever noticed how that bit of red frankfurt poking out the end of the bread roll looks like an erect…well, you know…"

"Sounds delicious!" Georg cried.

"But," Stefan went on while disappearing into the kitchen and returning with the aforesaid brains, canine appendages and salad, "isn't ethology close to eco-criticism?"

"It probably should be," Ronald said, "but eco-criticism has turned up as ecological hermeneutics in biblical studies."

"Is that where all the tree-huggers and wacky lefties have gone?" Ivy asked.

"Yeah," Ronald replied. "The basic idea is to be attentive to the voice and perspective of earth and nature in the text. The idea is to be focused on the non-human, or what they call other-than-human."

"How can you do that?" Gazza asked, "since humans are doing it?"

"And the ideas of 'earth' and 'nature' are put together in human thought and human texts," added Lisbett.

"You mean they're constructs," Geraldo suggested.

"Yes, that's what I was after," Lisbett said.

"OK," Ronald said, "these are some of the problems they face, but what would an ecological hermeneutics of Exodus look like?"

"The desert would be central," Fritz suggested.

"And of course the plagues," said Geraldo.

"And the crossing of the Reed Sea," Davey said.

"And the incidents of water from the rock," Ronald added.

"And quail and manna," Ivy said.

"OK, so there's a fair bit," Ronald said, "and when you start connecting them all you do get a different angle on things – even if many ecocritics are off with the pixies!"

"How old is this ecocriticism?" Fritz asked.

"As far as I can tell," Geraldo said, "it didn't really start to have an impact until the late nineties."

"At least queer criticism is a bit older than that," Stefan said. "It's still very tenuous in biblical studies, although I've had a bit of a go."

"And that follows on from gay and lesbian approaches," Ivy said.

"Yeah, and they don't always see eye to eye," Lisbett said. "Gays and lesbians tend to get a bit pissed off when straight people doing queer criticism conveniently hitch a lift after all the hard battles that were fought by gays and lesbians in the sixties and since."

"But," Ronald said, "how would a queer reading of the Exodus go?"

"Well, we can take a standard text and queer it," Stefan said, "you know, show up all its ambiguities over sexuality."

"Such as?" Lisbett asked.

"Oh, you know," Stefan replied, "when Moses goes up onto Sinai, what does Yahweh give him?"

"The commandments on two tablets of stone," Roland said.

"Oh, that's just a sideshow," Stefan said. "The main message comes in chapters 25, 26 and 27 of Exodus – three chapters of instructions for making the tent of meeting – down to the interior decorations of the tent, the making and arrangement of the gold and silver utensils, *and* – this is my favourite bit – the tassels and bells on the priests' robes."

"A queer Yahweh," Ronald said. "Hmmm...but isn't that grossly anachronistic?" Ronald asked.

"Of course," Stefan said, "but what interpretation isn't? And queer theory has a distinct political agenda – it sets out to disrupt normative biblical studies."

"It's more than that," Geraldo said. "It's not just a matter of disrupting biblical studies. Some of these approaches *do* have a real presence in the grubby world of politics."

"Like feminism, queer theory, ecocriticism, postcolonialism..." Ronald said.

"But that's what we do in the last chapter of *The Postmodern Bible*," Tini said. "Of course we have a political agenda!"

"The one on ideological criticism, you mean?" Ivy asked.

"Of course," Tini said, "that's where we deal with Fredric Jameson and Terry Eagleton, liberation theology, Norman Gottwald on the Hebrew Bible, Fernando Belo on the gospel of Mark, as well as African American biblical hermeneutics and indigenous readings..."

"It all sounds pretty Marxist to me," Ronald said, "damn Marxists, you'd think we'd have been rid of them by now, especially since the Berlin Wall came down!"

"True," Tini said, "but we also wanted to include African American and indigenous readings, especially of the Exodus..."

"Exodus would have to be a key text here, obviously," Gianna said, "but isn't it a bit suspect? You know, it is pretty much a myth, and yet liberation critics would love to have some historical basis in order to make use of it. On top of that the Exodus becomes the justification for the conquest of Canaan."

"That's where the indigenous readings are so valuable," Tini said, "since here in the United States the indigenous peoples have been cast as Canaanites so often."

"But why didn't you bite the revolutionary bullet," Geraldo said, "and call it Marxist criticism – most of the people you talk about are Marxists."

"Not sure..." Tini said.

"Do you think there's still some nervousness about Marxism in the United States," Ronald said. "Residue of the Cold War maybe..."

"Nervousness?" Geraldo said. "How about outright denial! Hence Ideological rather than Marxist criticism?"

"OK," Ronald said, "let's get down to it. What is the real edge of Marxism – or ideological criticism?"

"I reckon it's the way it holds so-called scientific or objective biblical scholarship to account for its own biases – you know, in terms of politics, class, gender, race and so on," Tini said. "Ideology shows us that we are never neutral, that we always have a distinct way of producing meaning for our lives."

"Is that what you would call a definition of ideology?" Ronald asked.

"I guess so," Tini said. "Ideological criticism would then be concerned with criticizing the processes – social and political – by which meaning is formed."

"What I like," Davey said, "are those great categories of mode of production, class conflict, ideology, base and superstructure."

"And I like the way Marxist criticism can't be separated from political commitment," Tini said.

"Like I said: damn Marxists, looks like they're everywhere!" Ronald said. "I really feel like a fag!"

The Americans present shot Ronald a strange look. There had been rumours of course, and he *would* tease people.

"No fags here, it seems to me," Geraldo said. The Americans were both relieved and a little disappointed. "You know," Geraldo went on, "a lot of Marxists have gone into postcolonial criticism."

"Do you think so?" Tini asked. "There are an awful lot of people interested in postcolonial criticism – more Marxists than ever there were. Maybe it's a gentler way of being introduced into the political side of biblical studies."

"Oh God," Ronald said, "not another post! Now we've got postmodernism, poststructuralism and postcolonialism. Do you think they're trying to tell us something?"

"Like what?" Tini asked.

"Maybe," Ronald said, "just maybe that something has passed, has been superseded?"

"I think it's more of a critical stance over against modernism or structuralism or colonialism," Tini replied. "We're conscious that something has shifted, that we're no longer in the midst of structuralism and colonialism and modernism. Sure, they're still with us in all sorts of ways, but the sign of the shift is that we now look at them very differently."

"But isn't the basic term postmodernism?" Ronald said. "It is, after all, *The Postmodern Bible*."

"True," Gazza said.

"But how do you understand that crucial term, postmodernism?" Ronald asked.

"Quite simply," Gazza said. "It's the culture you get with global capitalism."

"*What?*" Roland said

"Each type of economy has a type of culture that's most closely connected with it," Gazza said. "And by culture I mean a way of thinking about and living in the world. It's like a language, really. For example, with the slave economies of Greece and Rome everything was thought about in terms of politics. In the feudal economies of the Middle Ages, it was religion. And for us, in this new form of capitalism, it's postmodernism."

"But religion and politics are with *us* too!" Ronald said.

"Yes but they're no longer dominant," Gazza said, "and that's the key."

"But postmodernism, Gazza…give me a bit more," Ronald said.

"Well," said Gazza, "you get a lot of rubbish thrown around about postmodernism – like there's no truth or fact, that you say anything, that it's just a clever smoke screen – and some biblical scholars who should know better trot these things out. Apart from this rubbish, many people think of postmodernism as a style, in architecture or art or literature. If you look at city high-rise buildings, it's the ones that are all plexiglass and reflect their surroundings, or the buildings that seem to put a whole lot of styles together from different periods. But it's not just that. It's not just a fashion or a fad. I like the idea that postmodernism really is the best name for our culture as a whole. The profound changes that have taken place in capitalism – speculation on financial markets, freeing the dollar from the gold standard, the impact of the computer chip on all areas of life, the return of neo-liberal economic policies like the so-called 'free market,' the end of the Cold War – have had an impact on our culture. Maybe the best way to put it is that globalization is the flip-side of postmodernism. Just as the world is becoming more uniform through globalization – like Vodka in Australia, McDonald's in Mongolia, Californian oranges in Greenland, trans-national businesses with no base in any country – so also we find that postmodernism is the name of the first real global culture."

"Wow! What a mouthful!" Ronald said. "So postmodernism is the cultural form of McDonald's."

"That's not a bad way of putting it," Gazza said.

"So how does postcolonialism fit in?" Roland asked.

"It's another element of this huge change," Gazza said. "It also marks the shift that we all notice, but now from what used to be called the Third World. Postcolonialism really does follow on from the anti-colonial struggles of the 1950s and 1960s. India, Indonesia, the Philippines, a whole bunch of African nations and many more threw off colonial powers after World War II, and now these places have entered the global economy at some level. It also got a huge kick along with the rolling back of communism in Eastern Europe – the former Second World. It's often forgotten that this was a major factor in postcolonialism as well. Postcolonialism is, if you like, the collective name for all these developments."

"But postcolonial theory?" Roland asked, yet again.

"OK, that's the intellectual voice of all of these changes," Gazza said. "If we focus on literature, where postcolonial theory is strongest, we can see that all of the political and economic changes have obviously had an effect on the way literature is written, but also in the way we study it. I mean literature from outside the traditional focus of power around the Atlantic."

"Postcolonial theory sure has taken off," Ivy said, "not since feminism has an approach become so widespread and had such an appeal."

"Yeah," said Ronald. "As far as biblical studies is concerned, you find it in studies of the effect of the Bible and its translations in the whole era of European colonialism from the sixteenth to the twentieth century. You find it in studies of biblical times themselves, especially in reassessing the long history of colonial rule, from the Babylonians in the Hebrew Bible through to the Romans in the New Testament. But above all, you find it in the methods used to interpret biblical literature."

"But what's different about that?" Ivy interjected. "We knew that much of the Hebrew Bible came from a time of imperial domination, whether it was the Assyrians or Babylonians or Persians. And who doesn't know that the New Testament was written during the time of the Roman Empire?"

"Yes, but it makes a huge difference how you see the literature responding to those situations," Geraldo said, leaning back and pushing his long legs up against the coffee table. It weighed a ton and wasn't about to budge.

"OK, how?" Ronald said.

Geraldo paused, borrowing some of Davey's infinite patience. "There are some basic categories of postcolonial readings. But the best image for me is the Hottentot farting while he bows to the colonial master. In the same way biblical literature is full of underhand and subtle resistance to colonial power. It might pay lip service, but everywhere it gives hints of opposition."

"Yes, but *how*?" Ronald said.

"Two keys ideas come from Homi Bhabha," Geraldo said. "One is mimicry: resistant literature will mimic that of the colonial master, but its mimicry turns out to mock, ever so gently, the language and ideas of the master. It's like the child's game, where one child says everything another says until the first one says in sheer frustration '*Stop* copying me!' – knowing full well that the imitation is in fact mockery."

"And then of course the imitator says '*Stop* copying me!' " Ivy added.

"Yes," Geraldo laughed. "It's like using the master's tools against him. The second idea from Bhabha is hybridity: no position or idea or identity is ever pure, especially one of power. It will always have the seeds of subversion within it. If you examine it closely enough, a position of power shows deep internal contradictions against which it struggles to avoid its own collapse."

"Sounds like a politicized version of Derrida's deconstruction," Ronald said, gathering some empty bottles together to clear a space on the table, "or even Lacan's Real."

"No coincidence!" Geraldo said. "Bhabha draws his ideas from Lacan, and Gayatri Spivak, the second great theorist of postcolonialism, makes use of Derrida."

"But it's also like Marx's idea that a social system will eventually unravel due to its internal contradictions," Ronald said as the pile of bottles he had collected collapsed onto the floor.

"No coincidence again!" Geraldo cried, "since Edward Said, the third founding figure, relies on that great Marxist, Antonio Gramsci."

"And you could throw in the influence of Mikhail Bakhtin," Ronald said, "and his idea of a dialogical text – you know, two or more voices, one dominant and the other subversive. Or even Ernst Bloch, who read the Bible in much the same way well before postcolonial criticism. And he was a Marxist to boot!"

"So...Exodus?" Ivy said, disappearing into the kitchen.

"One way a postcolonial reading might work," Geraldo said, "is to look at the conflicting stories about the conquest of Canaan. Some texts, like Joshua 18:1 and 21:43–45, give us the picture of a very successful conquest, and then we find a text like Joshua 15:63, or chapter 13:1–7, or Judges 1, which give us a long list of peoples not conquered. And then we get to the end of Judges 1, in verse 34, and read: 'The Amorites pressed the Danites back into the hill country.' It's not just that there are peoples they didn't fully conquer or drive out. The Israelites actually have to resist attacks against them!"

"Isn't that just due to different sources?" Ronald said, dipping a potato chip into the bowl of sauce.

"That's an older and more restricted way of viewing the text," Geraldo said, "but we can also read these texts in terms of a quiet process of undoing the dominant image of a conquest with divine blessing."

"All very well," Ronald said. "But how is *that* a response to imperial dominance? Couldn't it be read as a more local struggle over the story? For instance, a scribe has to record some official story for the local king or governor. But he disagrees with it, and so he registers his disagreement in these sorts of ways."

"Perfectly plausible," Geraldo said, "but another level would be to read it as resistance to foreign domination. The locals will never give in; the control of the foreign power is never complete...especially if we see these stories coming out of the time of the Babylonian or Persian Empires."

"Or if we look at the New Testament," Tini said, "we can read the Apocalypse as a text of resistance against Rome. And we can translate the term *basileos theou* as Empire of God, rather than the older Kingdom of God – this is an empire that resists the Romans!"

"Wow!" Ronald cried. "This could run in all sorts of directions."

"You're not wrong," Geraldo said, "about the directions I mean. Postcolonial elements have been taken up in feminism, have provided a rallying point for contextual interpretations from Africa to Greenland, have influenced historians and literary critics, have given liberation theology a new lease of life, have given the crucial question of race a new angle..."

"There is one problem, though," Ronald said. "Aren't many of the leading postcolonial critics now based in First World universities?"

"Actually," Geraldo said. "That's the sign of a bigger problem that doesn't just happen with postcolonial critics. Long ago Terry Eagleton asked where the greatness of English literature and university life came from – in his book *Exiles and Émigrés*. And he found that nearly all the great figures came from outside England – Oscar Wilde, James Joyce, Joseph Conrad and on and on. They were drawn into the imperial centre and made their mark there."

"Or," Ivy said, "to put it crudely: England had the greatest universities because it had the biggest gunships."

"And if you look at the list of academics at any leading university in the United States," Ronald added, "you'll find that many if not most come from all over the world – India, China, Turkey, Australia, Europe... It's the same story as Imperial England."

"You've got to add another factor to that," Davey said. "Have you ever noticed how the key names in biblical studies before the 1960s were nearly all German? Julius Wellhausen, Hermann Gunkel, Martin Noth, to name a few out of many. And then from the 1960s the dominant voices are quite clearly from the United States."

"Is it because of the rise of the United States as a superpower after World War II?" Ronald asked.

"That's part of it," Davey said. "But there's also a specific historical reason. Most of the leading intellectuals fled Nazi Germany before and during the war, and many of them ended up in the United States – think of Einstein and Paul Tillich, for instance. Some returned home after the war, but many stayed and gave the US a huge intellectual kick along."

"The only real competition came from France," Lisbett pointed out. "There was Foucault and Derrida, Kristeva and Irigaray..."

"And even they got dragged across the Atlantic," Ronald said, "usually as regular visitors."

"Yes, but somewhere across the Atlantic," Ivy said, "their French political context was washed off. It just happens again and again when thinkers from Europe are picked up in the United States. They somehow get depoliticized."

"Actually," Ronald said, "what you mean is that the politics shift while they cross the Atlantic! In Europe Ted Kennedy would be a moderate conservative and in the Unites States he is a dirty liberal."

"On top of all of this," Ivy said, "you get what I'd call the Chosen People syndrome," Ivy said.

"You mean the idea that the United States calls itself or sees itself as God's Chosen People," Gazza said, "from the myth of the pilgrim fathers through to the idea we see now of some mission to save the world and the massive support of the state of Israel. I guess it's not for nothing that the ideas of Exodus and Promised Land turn up so often in the myths of the United States."

"It's more than that," Ivy continued, "since it shows up in an assumed universalism – you know, the idea that problems and questions in the United States are problems for the whole world. Something happens there – a building or two get blown up in New York, for instance – and suddenly it is a global catastrophe. There is such a propensity to generalize from these specific experiences, from your specific history – so the Chosen People syndrome. Or, if you like, the reverse: imperial blindness."

"That's right," said Geraldo. "The specific concerns of that strange little country between Canada and Mexico become the model for the whole globe. Think of it this way: when someone asks you 'seen any films recently?' do you not think of what is showing at the local cinema? And is it not invariably a Hollywood film? So much so that 'film' means Hollywood."

"Oh wow," said Georg, "so the whole story of Exodus in the Hebrew Bible shows up at this level. It's not just a matter of using it here and there for a bit of imperial propaganda, but it's just like the story of Exodus: this is the Chosen People, so this story is actually the story of the whole world."

"But is that the end of the story?" Ronald asked.

"Not at all!" Davey said. "There are a few straws in the wind that point to some profound changes. Let me put it this way: the destruction of the twin towers of the World Trade Centre in New York on 11 September is beginning to have an effect. I've met students looking for places to study for a PhD. Five years ago the United States would be their number one choice. Now it's not and they are beginning to look elsewhere. And there is the first trickle of academics who come from other countries wanting to get out of the US."

"So you think the US dominance of biblical criticism, among other things, is beginning to unravel?" Ronald asked.

"I think so," Davey said.

At that moment Ivy cried, "Enough *politics*! I've got a *headache* so big you could map it!"

"Why don't you try a glass of water and a sleep," Ronald suggested.

"Oh get lost!" Ivy said, "that's just what my father used to say! The solution to everything – headache, sore tummy, invasion by aliens – was a glass of water and a good sleep. The real *reason* I have a headache is because of this endless parade of methods. It just goes on and on and on: reader-response, rhetorical, semiotics, structuralism, poststructuralism, feminism, womanism, Marxism, ideological criticism, psychoanalysis, ecocriticism, indigenous hermeneutics, new historicism, postcolonialism, disability criticism, autobiographical criticism... When's it going to stop? When's it all going to stop?"

"It's like some massive explosion, with bits and pieces flying everywhere..." Georg said.

"And they don't seem to be slowing down," Stefan said, "today's fashion is tomorrow's boring old hat. It's like, poststructuralism, phew, that's *so* nineties!"

"It's a bit like the beer here," Geraldo said. "Don't get me wrong, I love beer, but we've got lagers and ales and bitters and porters and draughts and…"

"That's it!" Ivy said, "it *is* like a fashion, or like going to the supermarket. You just get endless choices of cheese or rice or bloody chocolate."

"Ohhhh, chocolate!" Tini said, "I *love* chocolate."

"Yes but," Ivy went on, "doesn't that mean that biblical studies, as a discipline, really is like any other commodity. It just proliferates into more and more products."

"That's a good piece of vulgar Marxism," Ronald said.

"Vulgar Marxism?" said Ivy.

"Oh, I don't mean my group of party animals, the Vulgar Marxists," Ronald said, "but connecting something like biblical studies directly with economics."

"Here's to Vulgar Marxists!" said Tini.

"To Vulgar Marxism!" said everyone, collectively, raising beer bottles, wine glasses and whatever container held something drinkable, hard or soft.

"But what's the answer?" Georg asked. "Do we just reject all of this newer stuff and hold onto the tried and true historical criticism?"

"Some would really love to," Ronald said.

"Yeah," Georg said, "there seem to be quite a few who feel they can just shrug off the new critical approaches of the last thirty years and stay with 'real' biblical scholars. So we can just go back to basic assumptions about history writing, such as historical positivism, and enjoy ourselves moving dates in one of two directions, backwards or forwards. *And* be concerned with the same questions of the last one hundred and fifty years – *why who wrote what and when*?"

"Why who wrote what when?" Ivy said, "that's not a bad description of historical criticism."

"But it *is* one of the marks of the impact of *The Postmodern Bible*," Geraldo said, "that those who hold onto historical criticism tend to call all of these newer approaches postmodern."

"And then we get the dismissals," Geraldo said. "Like: postmodern approaches are at best cute, but usually just trivial. Or: biblical historians don't need to concern themselves with the questions posed by philosophy or critical theory, for such historians know what they are doing. Or: literary studies don't engage people at a popular level; whether King David existed or not does. Or: complex literary interpretations don't sell, books about 'history' do. Or: postmodern interpretations are nothing more than intellectual masturbation."

"You're kidding," said Georg again.

"I kid you not," Geraldo said, "I've heard all of these."

"Oh, I like intellectual wanking," Ronald said, "in fact, I've been accused of it on more than one occasion."

"I'll vouch for that," Ivy said.

"OK," Fritz said, "but what's for the future? Where is it all going?"

"I think we're struggling for a new paradigm," Georg said. "The proliferation of methods often happens at times like this. And then there's reaction, a reassertion of what's tried and true. But historical criticism faced exactly the same battle. It emerged in the nineteenth century out of a welter of explorations, and then a conservative reaction set in and people started to assume it was a flash in the pan – until good old Julius Wellhausen."

"But are we really in search of a new paradigm?" Ronald asked. "Or will we have a plurality of methods that conflict with each other, form alliances, and enhance each other in the process?"

"I must admit I agree with Ronald," Fritz said.

"The problem with a dominant method," Lisbett said, "is that it really excludes and marginalizes other possibilities."

"Sure does," Tini said, "and it really becomes a way of control and domination – hegemony I think the word is."

"So it's either proliferation or putting the wagons in a circle?" Ronald suggested.

"Not quite," Geraldo said. "Shouldn't historical criticism become one method among many others, with its possibilities and shortcomings?"

"And maybe the way of showing up the shortcomings is in the interaction with other methods?" Ivy suggested.

"So it's not so much a liberal utopia," Fritz said. "You know, you're cool, I'm cool and we'll all sing Kumbaya."

"Much more a healthy conflict," Geraldo said. "A good argument or two never hurt anyone!"

"Get lost," Ronald said, "I never argue!"

"Oh, but I much prefer seeing the hand outstretched with the knife," Geraldo said, "than finding out that I have been knifed only when the blood trickles down my back."

"Or," suggested Fritz, "we need to come up with a way of accounting for all of this proliferation of methods."

"What do you have in mind?" Ronald asked.

"Well," Fritz said. "I've been toying with this idea for a bit, but it seems to me that we can think about three levels of biblical study – text, afterlives and metacommentary. The first one is focused on the text and all the things we can throw at it in order to understand it better. The second one concerns the myriad appropriations and interpretations of the text – you know, directly through interpretation, indirectly in culture, art, politics, law and on and on..."

"The Germans have a useful description for the second level," Ronald said. "They distinguish between *Rezeptionsgeschichte* – reception history or active and conscious interpretations – and *Wirkungsgeschichte* – the unconscious uses and passive echoes of the Bible in culture."

"Yes," Fritz said, "but these still assume the Bible is the *source* of all of these rereadings and echoes. It lies at the fountainhead, a bit like Eden in the biblical narrative. But there's another way to think about it, and that is like the Promised Land: the Bible then becomes the end point, and you have to work your way through all of the interpretations and echoes, since they influence us in so many ways."

"Eden and Canaan," Ronald said. "Hmmm... So at your second level we can go forwards *from* the text or backwards *to* the text. Is there any other way or are we locked into a two-way street."

"*That*," Fritz said, "would be one of the most interesting things to explore. Some have tried juxtaposing entirely unrelated things: a biblical text and, say, film come together in order to get them to spark in the friction. But I think it's only the beginning of a search for other possibilities."

"But what about your last level – what was it?" Ivy asked.

"Metacommentary," Fritz said. "That really is a call to account for all the methods that have been and might be used for interpretation. This is where we do get to play various methods off against each other, rather than claiming that one is the best, claiming that it will sweep the field and be the new paradigm."

"How do you do that?" Ronald asked.

"Oh," Fritz said, "you might bring postcolonial, historical critical, Marxist and feminist approaches together and test the insights and limits of each on your reading."

"A bit like Exodus," Ivy said, "where you might end up with a layering of readings in tension..."

"Now *that* would be fun," Geraldo said.

Already a discussion or two had begun in the corners, and from here the leaky house in Blackpool echoed to countless smaller discussions between two or three people. Lucidity had been slipping for a while – alcohol fortunately has that strange effect. Willy had fallen asleep on the couch, Ronald jumped up and down a few times to hear the alcohol swish around in his stomach, Geraldo began stomping on the floor to some decent rock music that he had put on the CD player, Ivy joined him, Fritz went for a walk down to the port, Georg went hunting for a hamburger, Gianna disappeared, Davey leant back and thought for a while, Lisbett produced some fantastic wine from a little stash in the corner, Gazza was itching for some exercise and thought about a swim, consoling himself with a basketball game on the television, Tini went to the kitchen to cook up a second batch of chicken livers, and Stefan had become a great lover of whale blubber salad. But *no one* was keen on the dog's dicks.

SELECT BIBLIOGRAPHY

Alter, Robert and Frank Kermode. *The Literary Guide to the Bible.* Harvard: Belknap, 1987.

Althusser, Louis. *The Future Lasts a Long Time.* Trans. Richard Veasey. New York: Vintage, 1994.

Bhabha, Homi. *The Location of Culture.* London: Routledge, 1994.

Bakhtin, Mikhail. *The Dialogic Imagination: Four Essays.* Trans. C. Emerson and M. Holquist. Austin, TX: University of Texas Press, 1981.

Bible and Culture Collective. *The Postmodern Bible.* New Haven, CT: Yale University Press, 1995.

Boer, Roland. *Marxist Criticism of the Bible.* Sheffield: Sheffield Academic Press, 2003.

Brenner, Athalya (ed.). *A Feminist Companion to the Bible.* Sheffield: Sheffield Academic Press, 1993-95.

—*A Feminist Companion to the Bible (Second Series).* Sheffield: Sheffield Academic Press, 1998-2001.

Cadwallader, Alan. "When a Woman Is a Dog: Ancient and Modern Ethology Meet the Syrophoenician Women." *The Bible and Critical Theory* 1.4 (2005). (www.epress.monash.edu.au/BC).

Cannon, Katie Geneva. *Katie's Canon: Womanism and the Soul of the Black Community.* London: Continuum, 1997.

Daly, Mary. *The Church and the Second Sex.* Boston: Beacon, 1986.

—*Gyn/Ecology: The Metaethics of Radical Feminism.* Boston: Beacon, 1990.

—*Beyond God the Father: Toward a Philosophy of Women's Liberation.* Boston: Beacon Press, 2nd edition, 1993.

—*Amazon Grace: Re-calling the Courage to Sin Big.* New York: Palgrave Macmillan, 2006.

Davies, Philip. *In Search of "Ancient Israel".* JSOTSup, 148; Sheffield: Sheffield Academic Press, 1995.

—*Scribes and Schools: The Canonization of the Hebrew Scriptures.* Louisville, KY: Westminster John Knox, 1998.

Derrida, Jacques. *Of Grammatology.* Trans. Gayatri Chakravorty Spivak. Baltimore, MD: The Johns Hopkins University Press, 1974.

—*Writing and Difference.* Trans. Alan Bass. Chicago: Chicago University Press, 1978.

—*Acts of Literature.* Ed. Derek Attridge. London: Routledge, 1992.

Dube, Musa. *Postcolonial Feminist Interpretation of the Bible.* Atlanta, GA: Chalice, 2000.

Eagleton, Terry. *Exiles and Émigres: Studies in Modern Literature*. London: Chatto & Windus, 1970.

Fiorenza, Elisabeth Schüssler. *In Memory of Her*. New York: Herder & Herder, 1984.

—*Searching the Scriptures. I. A Feminist Introduction*. New York: Herder & Herder, 1993.

—*Searching the Scriptures. II. A Feminist Commentary*. New York: Herder & Herder, 1994.

Foucault, Michel. *Discipline and Punish: The Birth of the Prison*. New York: Vintage, 1979.

—*The History of Sexuality* (3 volumes). New York: Vintage, 1990.

Freud, Sigmund. *The Standard Edition of the Complete Works of Sigmund Freud*. Trans. James Strachey *et. al.* New York: Vintage, 2001.

Gottwald, Norman K. *The Hebrew Bible: A Socio-Literary Introduction*. Philadelphia: Fortress, 1985.

— "Sociology of Ancient Israel". In *The Anchor Bible Dictionary*, VI (1992), 79-89.

—*The Hebrew Bible in its Social World and Ours*. Semeia Studies; Atlanta, GA: Scholars Press, 1993.

—*The Tribes of Yahweh: A Sociology of Liberated Israel 1050-1250*. Reprint Sheffield: Sheffield Academic Press, 1999. Original, Maryknoll: Orbis, 1979.

—"Political Activism and Biblical Scholarship: An Interview". Interviewed by Roland Boer. In Roland Boer (ed.), *Tracking the "Tribes of Yahweh": On the Trail of a Classic*. JSOTSup, 351; London: Sheffield Academic Press, 2002, pp. 157-171.

Gunkel, Hermann. *Genesis*. Göttingen: Vandenhoeck & Ruprecht, 3rd edn, 1910. 1st edn, 1901.

—*Die Psalmen*. Göttingen: Vandenhoeck & Ruprecht, 1926.

—*Einleitung in die Psalmen: die Gattungen der religiösen Lyrik Israels*. Göttingen: Vandenhoeck & Ruprecht, 4th edn, 1985. 1st edn, 1933.

—*Genesis*. Trans. Mark E. Biddle. Foreword by Ernest W. Nicholson. Macon, GA: Mercer University Press, 1997.

—*Introduction to the Psalms: The Genres of the Religious Lyric of Israel*. Completed by Joachim Begrich. Trans. James D. Nogalski. Macon, GA: Mercer University Press, 1998.

—*The Legends of Genesis: The Biblical Saga and History*. Trans. W. H. Carruth. Eugene, OR: Wipf & Stock, 2003.

Horsley, Richard A. *Archaeology, History and Society in Galilee: The Social Context of Jesus and the Rabbis*. Harrisburg, PA: Trinity Press International, 1996.

—*Bandits, Prophets and Messiahs: Popular Movements in the Time of Jesus*. Harrisburg, PA: Trinity Press International, 1999.

—*Hearing the Whole Story: The Politics of Plot in Mark's Gospel*. Louisville, KY: Westminster John Knox, 2001.

—*Jesus and Empire: The Kingdom of God and the New World Disorder*. Minneapolis: Fortress, 2002.

Irigaray, Luce. *This Sex Which Is Not One*. Trans. Catherine Porter and Carolyn Burke. Ithaca, NY: Cornell University Press, 1985.

—*An Ethics of Sexual Difference*. Trans. Carolyn Burke and Gillian C. Gill. Ithaca, NY: Cornell University Press, 1993.

Kristeva, Julia. *Revolution in Poetic Language*. Trans. Margaret Waller. New York: Columbia University Press, 1984.

—*Tales of Love*. Trans. Leon S. Roudiez. New York: Columbia University Press, 1987.

—*Strangers to Ourselves*. Trans. Leon S. Roudiez. New York: Columbia University Press, 1991.

—*New Maladies of the Soul*. Trans. Ross Guberman. New York: Columbia University Press, 1995.

Lacan, Jacques. *Ecrits: The First Complete Translation in English*. Trans. Bruce Fink. New York: W. W. Norton, 2005.

Lemche, Niels-Peter. *Ancient Israel: A New History of Israelite Society*. Sheffield: Sheffield Academic Press, 1988.

—*The Israelites in History and Tradition*. London: SPCK, 1998.

Moi, Toril (ed.). *The Kristeva Reader*. New York: Columbia University Press, 1986.

Morgan, Lewis Henry. *Ancient Society, or, Researches in the Lines of Human Progress from Savagery through Barbarianism to Civilization*. Chicago: C. H. Kerr, 1877. Reprinted New York: Gordon, 1987.

Moore, Stephen, and Fernando Segovia (eds.). *Postcolonial Biblical Criticism: Interdisciplinary Intersections*. London: T&T Clark, 2005.

Mowinckel, Sigmund. *The Psalms in Israel's Worship*. Trans. D. R. Ap-Thomas. Oxford: Basil Blackwell, 1962.

Noth, Martin. *Überlieferungsgeschichte des Pentateuch*. Stuttgart: W. Kohlhammer Verlag, 1948.

—*Geschichte Israels*. Göttingen: Vandenhoeck & Ruprecht, 1950.

—*The History of Israel*. Trans. P. R. Acroyd. London: Adam & Charles Black, 2nd edn, 1960.

—*Überlieferungsgeschichtliche Studie: Die sammelden und bearbeiten Geschichtwerke im alten Testament*. Tübingen: Max Niemeyer Verlag, 3rd edition, 1967.

—*A History of Pentateuchal Traditions*. Trans. and Intro. Bernhard W. Anderson. Atlanta, GA: Scholars Press, 1981.

—*The Chronicler's History*. Trans. H. G. M. Williamson. JSOTSup, 50; Sheffield: Sheffield Academic Press, 1987.

—*The Deuteronomistic History*. Trans. J. Doull *et. al.* JSOTSup, 15; Sheffield: Sheffield Academic Press, 1991.

Radford, R.R. *Womanguides: Readings toward a Feminist Theology*. Boston, MA: Beacon Press, 1996 [1985].

Said, Edward. *Orientalism*. London: Routledge & Kegan Paul, 1978.

Schaberg, Jane. *Resurrection of Mary Magdalene: Legends, Apocrypha, and the Christian Testament*. London: Continuum, 2004.

Spivak, Gayatri Chakravorty. *In Other Worlds*. New York: Routledge, 1988.

—*A Critique of Postcolonial Reason: Toward a History of the Vanishing Present*. Cambridge, MA: Harvard University Press, 1999.

Staley, Jeffrey L. *Reading with a Passion: Rhetoric, Autobiography, and the American West in the Gospel of John*. New York: Continuum, 1995.

Sugirtharajah, Rasiah S. *The Bible and the Third World: Precolonial, Colonial and Postcolonial Encounters*. Cambridge: Cambridge University Press, 2001.

—*Postcolonial Criticism and Biblical Studies*. Oxford: Oxford University Press, 2002.

Sugirtharajah, Rasiah S. (ed.). *The Postcolonial Bible*. Sheffield: Sheffield Academic Press, 1998.

Thompson, Thomas. *The Mythic Past: Biblical Archaeology and the Myth of Israel.* New York: Basic Books, 2000.

Tompkins, Jane. "Me and my Shadow." *New Literary History* 19.1 (1987), 169–78.

Trible, Phyllis. *God and the Rhetoric of Sexuality.* Philadelphia: Fortress, 1978.

—*Texts of Terror: Literary–Feminist Readings of Biblical Narratives.* Philadelphia: Fortress, 1984.

Wellhausen, Julius. *Prolegomena zur Geschichte Israels.* Berlin: Walter De Gruyter, 2001. Original publication 1878.

—*Prolegomena to the History of Israel, with a Reprint of the Article "Israel" from the* Encyclopaedia Britannica. Preface by W. Robertson Smith. Foreword to the Scholars Press Edition by Douglas A. Knight. Atlanta, GA: Scholars Press, 1994. Reprint of 1885 edn.

Whitelam, Keith. *The Invention of Ancient Israel: The Silencing of Palestinian History.* London: Routledge, 1996.

Yee, Gale. *Poor Banished Children of Eve: Woman as Evil in the Hebrew Bible.* Mineapolis: Fortress Press, 2003.

Subject Index

Printed in the United States
79164LV00001B/262-309

9 781845 531027